SHARED PERCEPTIONS

The Art of Marketing Real Estate Partnerships

SHARED PERCEPTIONS

The Art of Marketing Real Estate Partnerships

BY
NICK MURRAY

Editor
Robert A. Stanger

Publisher
Robert A. Stanger & Co.
Shrewsbury, New Jersey

Other Publications From Robert A. Stanger & Co.

Periodicals:

THE STANGER REGISTER
THE STANGER REPORT: A GUIDE TO PARTNERSHIP INVESTING
THE STANGER REVIEW: PARTNERSHIP SALES

Books:

HOW TO EVALUATE REAL ESTATE PARTNERSHIPS
STANGER'S PARTNERSHIP SPONSOR DIRECTORY
STANGER'S REAL ESTATE PARTNERSHIP PERFORMANCE WORKBOOK
TAX SHELTERS: THE BOTTOM LINE

Published by Robert A. Stanger & Co.
1129 Broad St., Shrewsbury, New Jersey 07701

Printed in the United States of America.

Library of Congress Catalog Card Number: 86-62821

ISBN 0-943570-09-3

This book is for
KAREN ELIZABETH, JOAN EILEEN
and
MARK PATRICK MURRAY,
who've never been able to explain to
their friends what their father does . . .

. . . and for
JONATHAN BARNETT,
friend

Contents

Acknowledgments

In trying to systematize the lessons of a sales career that now spans almost twenty years, I was reminded of the inexpressibly rich accumulation of good counsel, experience and help I've received during those years.

I was fortunate enough to go through the E.F. Hutton and Company training program in 1967 and to experience two devastating bear markets (1969–70 and 1973–74) in a fairly short time. Adversity is, after all, the greatest teacher, and what it taught me was that diversifying into "special products" was going to be critical to survival. It still is.

At Hutton, each in his own way, George Ball, Jerry Miller, Alan Rhein and Phil Rosenbaum helped me (usually in spite of myself) to learn my craft.

Marvin Brown taught me that there was, in its essence, such a thing as the sales process, and that question/objections handling and closing are matters of acquired skill, not of product knowledge. Since this book is, as you may have gathered, about the sales process *per se* more than about real estate sales, Marvin's contribution to it is very great.

Gordon Joblon was the bridge for me between Hutton and a struggling patchwork firm called (in 1975) Shearson Hayden Stone. Without that particular bridge at that particular moment in time . . .

My very strong commitment to the concept of networking can be traced to my experience with Shearson's "Magnificent Seven," which is the best example of that working arrangement I've ever seen or heard of. The "Seven" are Shelly Wilshinsky, Norman Fishbein, Alan Leavitt, Jim Hansberger, Len Leetzow, Ed Goldwasser and Evan Katz.

Since taking Aaron Hemsley's "Psychology of Maximum Sales Performance" course in 1983, I've done fairly extensive reading in the literature of behavior modification. But, I've never found anything that was even remotely as relevant to the securities salesperson's situation as is Aaron's program.

No one should consider a major new long-term prospecting effort without going through it.

At different times, and in different ways, Ira M. Koger of Koger Properties and Jack Crozier of Murray Financial have contributed to whatever real knowledge of real estate I may have. I hope this book repays their efforts in some way.

My colleagues at Bear, Stearns & Co., for whom I was consulting in 1985 when most of this book was written, were and are exceptionally supportive. I've acknowledged Jon Barnett's contribution on the book's dedication page. Mark Sandler, Livio Borghese and Ed Lowenthal have also helped an old dog learn some new tricks.

The greatest single contribution to this book has been Bob Stanger's. He encouraged me (at no small cost, since he already had someone working on a similar project when I showed up) and offered to become my partner in the book's publication. Most importantly, he edited the book, with perceptiveness and style, not once but twice: first on its completion at year-end 1985, and then again "post-Packwood."

And each time, when he took a meat cleaver to my purple prose, he reminded me that Hemingway had once attributed all his success to his editor. Well, Stanger's no Maxwell Perkins, and I sure as hell ain't no Hemingway. But, this is an infinitely better book than it would have been without him.

In the constancy of his probing, questioning and encouragement as I worked through this book, Harry Perlowitz, M.D., surely lived up to his name.

And, finally, thanks to the lady who insists on no acknowledgment, and who deserves it all.

N. M.

Author's Preface

We in the securities and financial planning industries now find ourselves on the brink of one of the great real estate buying opportunities of our careers.

Thanks to 1986's tax "reform," and its revolutionary attack on previously accepted concepts of real estate taxation, we're about to witness an uprecedented change in the way that property is developed, financed and traded.

The inevitable devastation of new apartment construction, which must result in significant rent increases, is only the most obvious consequence of this new legislation. As time goes on, the marketplace (unencumbered by a capital gains holding period, and focusing now on tax-sheltered cash flow) will reveal many other changes.

We will profit from these enormous changes only to the extent that we can, comfortably and conceptually, educate our clients and prospects to think in new ways about real estate. This will involve taking investors' long-established and well founded enthusiasm for real property, and gently channeling it into new investment configurations.

No one, at the depth of the last real estate depression in 1974–1975, could have envisioned the profits which blossomed just in the next five years. We will look back five years from now and observe precisely the same thing about the confusion and disarray in today's markets. And once again, the majority will ask, "How did we pass that up?"

Fear, overbuilding, a chaotic tax atmosphere and widespread uncertainty are the building blocks of every great buying opportunity. Turning all these phenomena to your advantage is what this book is about.

Use it well.

Nick Murray

Editor's Preface

With total lack of modesty, I have always thought the output of our research effort at Robert A. Stanger & Co. was without equal in the area of partnerships. I have personally edited this first book of Nick Murray's on marketing real estate partnerships, and I have the same enormous pride in the result. He has uniquely combined, subtly and unobtrusively, an understanding of real estate and a seductive appeal to excellence for every financial planner and investment salesperson, however experienced. The sales model provides a practical approach to prospecting and selling with just enough emphasis on behavior modification.

Murray combines the philosophy of the communication of investment products to clients with the essential philosophy of why real estate accomplishes important investment objectives. He weaves in a foundation of understanding real estate as an investment which transcends short-term trends and legislative change. The "post-Packwood" edit didn't require more than altering about three pages. Yet the resulting text is completely applicable to the post-1986 tax reform environment.

The purpose of this book isn't scripting of a "pitch" for starting salespeople. But, a sales model is completely laid out and adapted to five varieties of real estate partnerships. You won't find under any other cover the specific approaches to selling real estate partnerships that are presented here. This book gives you 99 and 44/100ths of what you need to know about essential agreement on the "concept," "the presentation," "tone," "answering objections" and the "close."

I can attest, after fighting over phrases and concepts as his editor, that Nick Murray is a "purist." His loyalty is to the communicator/salesperson, not the syndicator, wholesaler or investment research specialist. His in-the-trenches experience makes him speak to the feelings and reactions you experience when presenting investment products. At the same time, his approach is sympathetic, realistic and motivational. *Any* level communicator/salesperson will improve performance by listening to Nick's advice.

Best of all, this book is just like the author—lots of fun, with his unmistakable twinkle.

Robert A. Stanger

Introduction

Why Sell Real Estate Limited Partnerships

The great majority of American investors have enjoyed their most important success in real estate. In fact, it's safe to say that, **for many investors, a single real estate investment has produced a greater gain than all their other investments combined.**

Do these statements strike you as incredible? Of course not. You instinctively realized that we were referring to your own home.

The fact that you knew immediately what we were talking about and that what we said is true, lies at the very heart of why this book was written. **People simply love to invest in good real estate** because their personal experience, and that of so many people they know, has been so favorable.

Yet, beyond owning a home (and perhaps a vacation house or condominium) most investors' access to good real estate investments is very limited. Why? Serious players in the complex world of investment-grade real estate require lots of cash, not to mention time and expertise.

Enter the Real Estate Limited Partnership (hereafter referred to as the RELP). The unique ability of the RELP to offer passive investors the full range of real estate benefits, while completely relieving them of the management headaches, has led to one of the great success stories in the history of American finance.

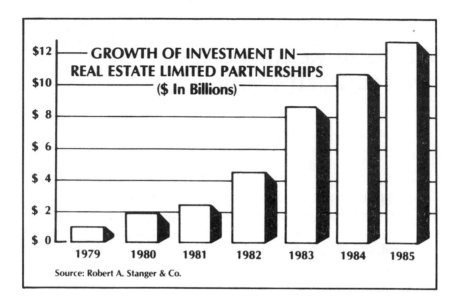

This book was written for the securities salesperson or financial planner who wants to be a part of this great growth phenomenon, or who would like to be more effective at communicating his enthusiasm successfully to clients.

Perhaps you are bewildered by the variety of RELPs with which, increasingly, you seem to be bombarded: public and private, equity and mortgage funds, leveraged and all-cash, new construction and mature properties, glitzy resort hotels and little neighborhood shopping centers. Maybe what's left you scratching your head is the mind-numbing complexity of the prospectus, or all the conflicting jargon you hear from the sponsors.

Never mind. The very things that are making you a good communicator/salesperson of all the other investment media in which you deal will make you equally effective in RELPs, if you'll just relax and let those skills take over.

And there are ample reasons for making the effort to become a skillful salesperson of RELPs. They go very far beyond the idea of just getting your piece of the rapidly expanding RELP sales pie.

- Real estate is a superior investment in a wide variety of economic environments. Put another way, you don't have to be right about economic trends to make a successful investment in real estate.

  Here's a rather startling chart of returns on real estate and other investments for the period 1951–1978.

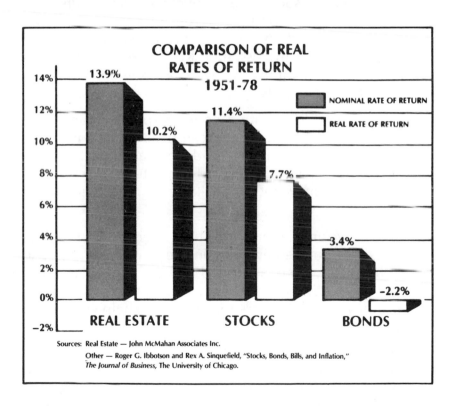

COMPARISON OF REAL
RATES OF RETURN
1951-78

NOMINAL RATE OF RETURN

REAL RATE OF RETURN

REAL ESTATE 13.9% 10.2%

STOCKS 11.4% 7.7%

BONDS 3.4% -2.2%

Sources: Real Estate — John McMahan Associates Inc.
Other — Roger G. Ibbotson and Rex A. Sinquefield, "Stocks, Bonds, Bills, and Inflation," *The Journal of Business,* The University of Chicago.

The interesting thing is that the period covered by the chart is fairly evenly divided between exceptionally low inflation (1951–1964) and very high inflation (1965–1978). So, if your question is, "Does real estate outperform stock and bonds in periods of low inflation," or "Does real estate outperform stocks and bonds in periods of high inflation?" the answer would clearly seem to be "yes" to both.

- Real estate answers so many different investor needs. Long-term growth of capital, current income that can rise, superior rate of return—all are among the highest investor priorities, and all are uniquely characteristic of real estate.

- RELPs come in such wide product varieties. At first, this fact may seem to be part of your problem rather than part of the solution. But the plain fact is that being conversant with the essential RELP sales process gives you an infinite variety of real estate solutions you can apply to client needs.

- Sophisticated RELPs are a peerless source of access to the substantial investor. He can hear about any stock, bond, annuity or mutual fund from anyone, but your RELP product line (particularly private transactions) is unique and may not be available from another firm's broker.

- RELPs have an extraordinarily high referral potential. The best client you can ever obtain is one who came to you at the suggestion of a satisfied friend. People like to talk about attractive real estate investments they've made, and they're usually more than willing to help you spread the word.

- RELPs are very low-maintenance vehicles. Since they can't be quoted in the newspaper every day, people aren't always calling you up to ask, "Why was it down/up yesterday?" Good RELP sponsors do an effective investor relations job, and you can piggy-back your subsequent sales efforts on their reports.

- RELPs aren't particularly price-sensitive. What's more disheartening than having a prospect shop your stock, bond, or life insurance idea around, and find he can buy it "cheaper" at some discount source? Never mind that it was your idea, or that he won't get the same follow-up and personal concern— he bought on the issue of price. Price is usually *not* a competitive issue in RELPs.

None of these very compelling reasons to sell RELPs may be news to you. On the contrary, you may find in them the all-too-familiar frustration of wondering how to turn compelling reasons more effectively to your advantage.

If that's the case, you're reading the right book. On the other hand, if you've a burning desire to learn what RELPs *are,* and the nuts and bolts of how they work, you're most assuredly reading the wrong book. Because *Shared Perceptions* is your one guide to the great truth about selling these diverse and fascinating investments:

SYSTEMATIC SELLING EFFORTS ALWAYS LEAD TO BETTER PRODUCT KNOWLEDGE; IT NEVER WORKS THE OTHER WAY AROUND.

1

What Are You Selling?

At the outset, let us encourage you to try to forget, as nearly as possible, everything you've learned about RELPs. That's because, for most people, the seeds of the reasons you're not reaching your full potential are already sown in the things you're now saying and doing.

The ideal student for a tennis pro is someone who's never had a racquet in his hands. He hasn't picked up any bad habits. That's why your best chance to get the most out of this book is to let it start you off at ground zero. You may find out that it's not so much the things you're doing and saying that are holding you back. **Your basic assumptions about the RELP sales process may be wrong.**

So, start with the simple question, "What am I selling?" Was your answer any combination of "real estate," "long-term capital gain," "tax shelter," "income," and things like that? We can assure you that you're already heading down the wrong road, because first of all, as in every other human activity that involves you and other people, **you are selling yourself.**

SELL YOURSELF FIRST

This is of paramount importance in the RELP sales process. The reason: People simply do not bring to RELPs a body of prior investment knowledge (as they do, for instance, in stocks and bonds), or a feeling that they understand the basic concept (as they do in life insurance and CDs).

The act of launching into an enthusiastic description of why a particular RELP is such a superior product is already doomed. The people you're talking *to* may not have any frame of reference for what you're talking *about*. Then why are you doing it? Far too often, the honest answer is: Because that's the presentation the wholesaler gave me, and I thought it sounded very good.

You were both right. **The presentation does sound good, but only after you've established a basic, shared perception of why you're even talking about real estate in the first place.** And even before that happens, you have to create and maintain an active feeling of real confidence in you on the part of the people you're talking to.

Even the brightest investor is always going to have a sense that he doesn't fully understand all the inner workings of a RELP. He is therefore going to arrive at a point in your conversations where he concludes, in effect: (1) that he's heard about as much information as he can process; (2) that he has a general (if undefined) feeling that the transaction is well thought out; and (3) that he's decided to believe that your representations as to the probable outcome of the deal are reasonably accurate. He is going to make the investment. Please note that:

THE CRUCIAL EVENT IN THE SALES SEQUENCE IS THAT THE PROSPECT DECIDES TO BELIEVE YOU.

When you think about it, what else could it be? You are *never* going to be able to give him enough real estate information to enable him to reach a fully informed, intellectual decision to invest in the transaction. (That doesn't, however, stop an awful lot of salespeople and planners from trying — to their sorrow.)

If you can understand that belief in you is the basis of decision, and accept that fact, you've already made your first big breakthrough. The simple fact is that people don't buy RELPs from people they *understand;* people buy RELPs from people they *believe.*

As in all other areas of investment, **you're going to be most successful selling those RELPs you believe in the most.** Trying to be an expert in all of them, so that you can intelligently compare and contrast them, and fit each one minutely to each client's varying needs . . . it'll never work. And it shouldn't have to.

Most very good stockbrokers say that there are six to ten companies that they can follow closely at any given time. They don't feel they have to know *all* the stocks, so they can proudly claim that their six are the "best." They're saying, in effect, "Here's the kind of professional I am. I know my limitations. I can only diligently follow six stocks at a time. I like these industries. There is good chemistry between me and management. If you're comfortable with that, there's a good chance you'll be comfortable with me. If not, maybe you should be talking to somebody else."

Your own confidence and professionalism are going to be the deciding factors in the RELP sales process. That should be your essential attitude in selling RELPs. You should be able to project the perception that your clients are, when all is said and done, buying you. And, through you, they're buying the people who sponsor the RELP. Because, and don't let the client ever lose sight of this, **the real estate business comes down to people.** The identity, character, business acumen and financial strength of a RELP's general partner are the deciding issues in the success or failure of the transaction — not the bricks, sticks, location, mortgages or any of that "hard information."

Don't you forget it, either. If your clients are investing their confidence in you, then your enthusiasm and depth of feeling for a sponsor and his transactions are the most powerful tools you have going for you — not the facts, numbers and ratios that you know.

It all comes down to you. The client must sense that you care about him, that you're trying as best you can to have him invest in a good situation, that you feel strongly about the quality of the investment and the strength of the people behind it . . . then that client's main concerns have been answered. And if he doesn't sense your conviction and sincerity, then no amount of factual material is going to get you where you want to go.

SELL THE CONCEPT

The second thing you have to be selling at all times is what we'll call, for want of a better term, THE CONCEPT.

When a client sits down to talk to you about, say, a mutual fund, he already has THE CONCEPT: A professional money manager is going to accept the client's capital, commingle it with the money of thousands of other investors, and manage the account toward some specific investment goal.

That's an enormous shared perception upon which to build your sales presentation, isn't it?

But, can you remember when short-term money market funds were developed in the early 1970s? What an amazingly difficult sales job . . . and it didn't even cost the customer a commission! Why was it such a struggle? Because the client didn't yet understand THE CONCEPT.

When you sit down with any client to talk about a RELP, you'd better be prepared, right off the bat, to give him THE CONCEPT: a single, central perception that fixes in his mind exactly what this investment is trying to do for him.

Chances are, when you were a freshman in college, you had to take a composition course. And you may have had to buy a book called *The Elements of Style* by William Strunk, Jr., edited by E.B. White. In his introduction, White says:

"Will (Strunk) felt that the reader was in serious trouble most of the time, a man floundering in a swamp, and that it was the duty of anyone attempting to write English to drain this swamp quickly and get his man up on dry ground, or at least throw him a rope."

If you just substitute "prospect" for "reader" in that sentence, and "the RELP salesperson" for "anyone attempting to write English," you'll have a pretty accurate understanding of how urgent it is to give a prospect THE CONCEPT.

For example, suppose you have a pension plan client who's been loading up on high quality corporate and government bonds. You want the trustees of the plan to purchase a fair-sized participation in an all-cash RELP (one that does not borrow). Now remember, all their attitudes and analytical tools are bond-oriented: They think in terms of the coupon, maturity dates, quality ratings, yield-to-maturity, etc.

Now, all of a sudden, you want them to abandon all that familiar territory and sail off into a world where they don't know exactly what each year's cash yield will be. They don't know exactly when the investment will "mature." They don't know what the value of the investment will be when it's sold. Looked at in this way, your chances of selling this account seem to cover the whole spectrum between slim and none . . . unless you're prepared to go head-on into THE CONCEPT:

"Gentlemen, you've assembled, on behalf of the beneficiaries of this plan, as high-quality a bond portfolio as I've ever seen, and you are to be congratulated for it.

In constructing this portfolio, you've covered all the bases that bonds can cover: safety, competitive current income, and diversified maturities. Now, I'd like you to consider the one thing that no fixed-income portfolio can ever really defend you against: inflation.

Inflation isn't something people are very worried about right now . . . and maybe that, in itself, should tell us something. But you are investing for a person's whole working lifetime. And, when you retire, how many dollars you end up with doesn't matter; only what those dollars will buy matters.

So, I'd like you to consider doing what the largest, most sophisticated pension plans do: Include income-producing real estate in your portfolio.

Real estate, in my experience, is the one income-producing asset whose future income stream and future value can continue to rise in any kind of economic environment. I know that, in buying real estate, you give up some of the certainty and the liquidity you are used to in bonds.

But, as far as liquidity goes, you shouldn't even consider buying real estate to the point where it threatens the liquidity needs of your plan. And as for certainty . . . well, gentlemen, the biggest uncertainty we face is the purchasing power of the dollar years from now.

I've chosen an all-cash real estate partnership for your consideration. I prefer this kind of real estate participation for a pension plan, because the classic risk of real estate investing, foreclosure, isn't a factor here. All-cash real estate partnerships do not mortgage properties.

The other great benefit of all-cash real estate is cash flow. Once occupancy reaches 28% to 30% of the property, operating expenses are covered. Over that level all the rent falls right to the bottom line and becomes cash flow to your pension plan. Cash that you can reinvest, or use to pay benefits.

Gentlemen, if this concept seems reasonably sound to you, may I tell you some of the details?"

No matter how slowly and deliberately you speak, this presentation can't possibly take more than two or three minutes. But do you see how it raises the level of the conversation? Do you see that the nuts and bolts of the investment have taken a back seat to the overriding conceptual fit of the RELP to the investment need?

Whether you're talking to a $2,000 IRA prospect or a Fortune 500 CEO with $500,000 of investable income burning a hole in his pocket, start with . . . THE CONCEPT.

Oddly enough, the "bigger" the prospect, the less time and attention he can give to an encyclopedic recitation of all the details of the transaction, and the more he appreciates the intelligence of someone who cared enough to boil it all down to a two-minute précis. A wise man said there are only two commodities in the world: time and money. The prospect who has the time for endless, agonizing detail probably doesn't have the money. The prospect with a substantial amount of money has rather pressing demands on his time.

Once you've got a prospective investor comfortable with and agreeing to THE CONCEPT, you're more than halfway home. And the converse is at least equally true: Without a central, governing concept to hang his hat on, your client will never be able to process all the details of a transaction to the point where he'll want to own it.

SELL EXPOSURE

There's one more thing, under the heading of what you're selling, that we should cover right now. Actually, this one has as much to do with what you are *not* selling as it does with what you are selling. Simply stated:

SELL EXPOSURE, NOT PROOF.

If you don't immediately see what we mean, go back to that presentation of THE CONCEPT for the pension fund. Where, in that presentation, does it say how much the yield will be three years from now? Where does it say how much the properties will appreciate? Where does it say when they'll be sold?

Right . . . it doesn't allude to any of those estimates, because they are unknowable facts. What it says is: Income-producing real estate is your best shot at inflation-hedged income and capital values, and you ought to be exposed to those potentialities with some percentage of your assets.

That's all. If you let your mission, in the sales interview, become maneuvered into the mode of trying to prove that this particular RELP will, over the next seven years, outperform a 7-year, AA corporate bond, you've had it. Why? Because you've let yourself be cast in the ultimate false position: You're trying to *prove* that which can't be proven.

The more numbers and projections there are in the prospectus or offering memorandum, the greater the danger that you'll be drawn into a no-win argument about those numbers. That's why private placements are even more dangerous, with respect to the "burden-of-proof syndrome," than are public deals. Whenever you're presenting a RELP with a lot of detailed projections (or even a RELP with no projections but a very detailed track record), try to remember to say something like:

> "Now, of course, the actual results of this particular RELP are going to conform exactly to these projections (or track record figures) . . .
> Unless they happen to turn out either higher or lower."

Even if you do not immediately have the courage to say these words right out loud to the client, at least remember to say them to yourself. You don't get paid nearly enough to predict the future. But you surely should know how to select the best practical opportunity for the client to fulfill his goals. Given those financial goals, **you believe you're showing your client the single best opportunity you can find for him at this**

time. And, your attitude just has to be: If that's not enough, my friend, you have to look elsewhere.

SUMMARY

You are selling:

- **Yourself, first and foremost.**
- **THE CONCEPT.**
- **Exposure, not proof.**

2

What You Need to Know

Brigadier General Charles E. (Chuck) Yeager must be having an awful lot of fun these days, and heaven knows he's earned it.

It was October 12, 1944, when Chuck Yeager, at the age of 21, took on and shot down five German fighter planes in succession. Just over three years later, on October 14, 1947, he became the first man to fly an airplane faster than the speed of sound. And for another twenty years, he was on the cutting edge of American fighter aircraft testing.

But it wasn't until 1979, when Tom Wolfe's book, *The Right Stuff*, rocketed to the top of the best-seller lists, that Yeager began to get the recognition he deserved. Since then, the movie made from Wolfe's book (in which Yeager does a typically dry, funny and nearly anonymous turn) has been followed by the pilot's own autobiography. And we've finally come to recognize a real American hero.

Yeager was the preeminent test pilot of his time, and his time saw us from propeller flight to a manned landing on the moon. And yet, the remarkable fact is that, throughout his long and distinguished career:

**NOBODY EVER ASKED CHUCK YEAGER
TO BUILD AN AIRPLANE.**

Well, come to think of it, that's not very remarkable at all. Yeager did what he did better than any man alive. So no one would have dreamed of asking him to do something else. The same can be true, in some small way, for all of us.

So, before you take even one more step along the road to becoming a successful RELP salesperson:

ASK YOURSELF,
"WHAT CAN MY CLIENTS AND PROSPECTS
REASONABLY ASK ME TO DO?"

It would be counterproductive to suggest that there's a universally valid answer to that question. But asking the question of yourself will start to clarify some central issues.

If you're a securities salesperson, or a financial planner who nets 60% of your gross commissions or less, then for purposes of this discussion your predominant function is one of communication and sales. If, on the other hand, you work on a fee basis, or operate so independently that your net commissions approximate the total gross credit, your role may indeed encompass due diligence and product selection. For the great majority of readers who see themselves in the communication/sales segment of our profession, this distinction is of crucial importance.

The commission-based RELP salesperson simply cannot be the technical expert on the myriad of tax and economic factors that make up the universe of RELPs. Yet the salesperson often backs himself into a corner where he's unconsciously saying, "Well, if I don't understand all that stuff, I don't *deserve* to be making a lot of RELP sales." Psychologically, and from a practical business standpoint, that way of thinking is unsound and extremely dangerous.

The successful RELP salesperson has to start from the position of setting his own professional agenda and not letting his clients and prospects set the agenda for him. This conscious defining of one's role is critical in every aspect of a securities sales career, and especially important when you're tackling a new product for which your prior experience does not help you very much.

Think of it this way: The greatest life insurance planner in the world never pretends he's an actuary. Chances are the best stockbroker you know would be the first to tell you he's not a securities analyst.

But the minute you start thinking about trying to become a proficient RELP salesperson, you can be instantly daunted by the tremendous weight of real estate knowledge you don't yet have.

Beware! It is absolutely fatal to think of product knowledge as being a precondition of a successful sales effort. The whole point of this book is that the opposite is true: **What's most important right now is what you do, not what you know.**

AVOID PRODUCT KNOWLEDGE PARALYSIS

Let's talk for a while about what product knowledge *can't* do, so that we have a clearer, healthier picture of how important product knowledge is.

Most importantly, product knowledge is no defense against being asked a question you can't answer. Yet, that's just how a lot of salespeople try to use it. RELP products, particularly the larger, more sophisticated private placements, put the salesperson in a position where he may be asked a question he can't answer. And, everyone naturally fears that this lack of knowledge will demean him professionally in the eyes of the client, or the client's advisors.

The fear of not knowing the answer is paralyzing many potentially fine RELP salespeople. This fear often leads to an unconscious defensive attitude in which the salesperson says, "First, I'm going to acquire so much knowledge about this product that nobody will ever ask me a question I can't answer. That way I'll never look dumb in front of my best clients and prospects.''

You cannot win with this attitude because you are setting a goal which is unobtainable. Think of the old mathematical conundrum: A man is standing thirty feet from a wall; he walks halfway to the wall, and stops; then he walks half the remaining distance to the wall, and stops again. How many times will he repeat this process before he reaches the wall? The answer, of course, is that he never reaches the wall. By definition, every time he moves, he only goes halfway to the wall.

In this analogy, the wall is "enough" product knowledge so that you are never stumped. You cannot reach that point. You'll never know enough so that you can't be asked a question you can't answer.

In fact, you cannot even begin to arm yourself with answers for investors' questions and problems until you go out and start making a lot of sales presentations. You must actually begin to hear the real hopes, fears, concerns, suspicions and misapprehensions that real clients have. No amount of preparation can do that for you. You simply cannot learn to hit major league pitching by reading a book, or watching a tape. You just have to step up to the batter's box, stand at the plate and take your cuts.

Your mind-set has to be: I'm presenting a high-quality RELP to my prospects because I sincerely believe that this transaction genuinely meets their needs and merits inclusion in their financial plans. I am paid to communicate that "fit" in a sufficiently convincing way to cause them to take action. Matters of fact and law will *always* require clarification. As I get more and more experience, my knowledge of those issues will grow. But in the meantime, the technical people in my firm and with the RELP sponsor are more than happy to pitch in on a conference call if I need help. I can concentrate on becoming the great communicator/salesperson I intend to be without fear of facts that I don't know yet.

Perhaps the whole problem can be put in perspective for you if, right here and now, we offer you the following 24-month, 240-presentation warranty:

**FOR THE NEXT TWO YEARS
OR FOR YOUR NEXT 240 RELP PRESENTATIONS
(WHICHEVER COMES LATER),
YOU WILL ALWAYS BE ASKED A QUESTION
YOU CAN'T ANSWER.**

There, isn't that refreshing? Doesn't that take a tremendous amount of anxiety out of the RELP sales process for you? Just accept that proposition (because the rest of this book is going to be very valuable to you if you do), and you can instantly stop worrying about everything you don't know. Chapters 13 and 14, "Questions and Answers," will show you how to make concrete, tactical plans for handling the inevitable question you can't answer and turning the exercise to your advantage.

USE YOUR POWERS OF SIMPLIFICATION

Even the brightest potential RELP salesperson can wander off aimlessly into the trackless desert of product knowledge thinking that RELPs are meaningfully more complex than the other investment media in which he deals. This problem just falls apart the moment you look directly into it. Still, the amount of damage done by this perception is really incalculable.

The thought process is articulated as follows (but not nearly in so few words): I understand stocks and bonds. Stocks and bonds are simple. I understand life insurance and annuities. They are simple. But, I don't understand RELPs. RELPs are complex. I have to learn much more about them before I can sell them.

The notion that RELPs are complex is an illusion. And the idea that those other financial media are simple is equally groundless. What's actually happening here is that, over the years, you've easily (and unconsciously) developed enormous powers of *assumption* and *simplification,* which enable you to take vastly complex investments and communicate their essences to your clients.

You would never try to convince a prospect to invest in a single-premium deferred annuity (SPDA) by explaining the legal reserve life insurance system to him, even though that's the financial and legal basis upon which the soundness of SPDAs rests.

If you thought a client should own a thousand shares of IBM, you wouldn't try to explain to him the business plan and financial structure of the International Business Machines Corporation. He wouldn't understand those things, nor necessarily see any direct connection with the stock's price movement. Neither, in all likelihood, would you.

The prospect who should invest $25,000 in a new general obligation bond of your home state neither needs nor wants a detailed analysis of your state's finances, budget process, and fiscal politics. You tell him the coupon, the price, the quality rating, the maturity date, the current yield and why you think the investment is right for him. That ought to take about a minute and a half.

All these investments are very far from simple. They just *seem* simple to you because you have the instinctive ability to filter out an enormous amount of technical detail that's extraneous to the communication and sale.

RELPs are almost infinitely simpler than most other investments. First of all, they're relatively small. A $50-million RELP is a fairly big deal, but a $50-million bond financing is an odd lot. Second, RELPs are very narrowly focused. A private placement generally owns one property. Even a fairly large public deal rarely has more than a dozen properties, and those properties usually have a number of very identifiable common features. The general partner will be only too happy to tell you what those features are.

The strategy for making money in a RELP will usually rest on a very small number of economic and tax issues. Never mind that the prospectus or offering memorandum rambles on for 200 stylized, legalistic and ultimately incomprehensible pages. **A RELP with more than three absolutely critical issues is the exception, not the rule.**

But when you start talking about a RELP, all your remarkably effortless powers of simplification may seem to fly out the window. Instead, you'll find yourself stumbling around in a quagmire of mortgages, cap rates, demographics, guarantees, fee structures, and sharing arrangements. This entire host of minutiae leaves the client only slightly more bewildered than you are. And you still think what you need is more product knowledge? Nonsense!

Remember the fable of the Fifty-first Dragon? Seems there was this new knight who graduated at the bottom of his class. All the other graduates had picked the best jobs for knights: One was off questing for the Holy Grail, another was in charge of rescuing damsels in distress, and so forth. All that was left for our hero was battling fire breathing dragons, the very thought of which turned his knees to jelly.

So, he went to Merlin and said, "Either you give me some magic charm to make me effective against dragons, or I'm going to wash out of the program." Merlin rummaged around his workshop and came up with an old, rusty, battered helmet. He gave it to our hero and said, "Kid, this is it. Wear this magic helmet when you go out to slay a dragon and you'll be invincible."

Our boy clapped that helmet on his head, went out there, and wiped out every dragon in six counties. He killed 'em right-handed, left-handed, two at a time, chopped them up and brought home dragonburgers in Saran Wrap.

Two months later, when he'd killed his fiftieth dragon, he took Merlin out for a celebratory lunch. After they'd knocked back a lot of mead, Merlin told him the truth: The helmet was just an old piece of junk. Merlin could see that the kid had the natural ability to be the best dragon-slayer in the major leagues *if* he could get over his irrational fears. So Merlin told him the helmet was charmed and let nature take its course.

(Just to finish the story, our hero then went forth without the helmet, and the fifty-first dragon had him for brunch. Never mind that.)

The moral of the story is that **what's stopping you from huge success in selling RELPs may be entirely inside your own head.** You may be suspending those terrific powers of simplification that make you a great salesperson of the other investments in which you deal. The major opportunity with respect to this totally imaginary issue of "complexity" is to **stop defeating yourself.** Accept, from this moment on, that:

> **RELPS ARE PRETTY SIMPLE . . .**
> **IT TAKES A TRULY CREATIVE SALESPERSON**
> **TO LOSE IT**
> **AND MAKE THEM COMPLEX.**

COMMUNICATE BENEFITS, NOT FEATURES

Another genuinely destructive result of a whole lot of product knowledge is to make you comfortably and vocally conversant with what a RELP *is,* ignoring what a RELP *does.* Of all the really bad things that can happen to you, few are worse.

An old salesman's maxim holds that no one in our industry is paid for what he knows, only for what he does with what he knows. The flip side of that perception is, if possible, even more true:

> **NO ONE EVER BOUGHT AN INVESTMENT**
> **FOR WHAT IT IS . . .**

PEOPLE ONLY BUY AN INVESTMENT
BECAUSE OF WHAT IT WILL DO FOR THEM.

This breathtaking truth lies at the heart of one of the greatest sales philosophies ever developed: the Xerox Sales Training Course. If you are only glancingly acquainted with the Xerox system, you may wrongly write it off in three facile words: "features and benefits."

But the power to understand, appreciate and use the critical distinction between features and benefits differentiates the great RELP salesperson from all the floundering failures he leaves in the dust.

People who throw themselves wholeheartedly into the quest for more product knowledge tend to end up knowing what RELPs *are*. The salesperson who focuses on what RELPs *do* for his clients will probably be comfortably retired when his more intellectually rigorous colleague is still trying to solve the riddle of what each type of RELP is. The intellectual grows old constructing tables of features comparing all-cash RELPs and participating-mortgage RELPs for his pension client (who has $2,689 to invest).

No great generalization about selling can ever be entirely correct (which is why selling, like baseball, is such an accurate metaphor for life). But you can stake your career on the perception that the communicator/salesperson who can tell his clients, with a lot of warmth and feeling, what a RELP is trying to *accomplish* is virtually assured of success. And you can be equally sure that the person who knows, down to the ground, what a RELP *is,* and how it works, may end up standing on the platform, wondering how the train managed to leave without him.

TELL A LOVE STORY

The last, most dangerous form of "product knowledge paralysis" is saying: The first thing I have to do, before I start trying to sell RELPs, is to learn which one fits exactly which investment need . . . *then* I'll know how to sell with confidence. The "justification" is that there are an incredible variety of RELPs and an infinite variety of client needs.

Six months later, the fellow who follows this line of reasoning will be found slumped over his desk, his forehead resting on the legal opinion page of a RELP offering memorandum. Although he won't have noticed (because it isn't much different from the way he'd been living), he's actually passed away. And everybody in the office always liked him, so nobody's had the heart to tell him yet. On his calendar for next Tuesday are the aggressive words: "Make first RELP sale."

Seriously, the psychology of learning the ins and outs of a dozen RELP products before you begin to sell is an absolute guarantee that you'll never, ever become a proficient RELP communicator/salesperson. No one is *asking* you to be an expert able to compare all kinds of RELPs. Clients expect you to know about a RELP that has a much-better-than-even chance of performing well *for them*. (Remember that someone who's looking for you to do much more is, at worst, casting you in the false position of asking you to offer "proof." At best, he's setting the agenda, and you've already promised yourself this is *your* territory.) Learn to understand the benefits of a very few RELPs across the spectrum of client needs.

In a later chapter, we'll suggest that if you know and love one leveraged equity RELP, one participating mortgage fund (or all-cash equity RELP) and one publicly traded REIT, you'll be able to cover 75% of all the client needs you'll run across in your first year of offering RELPs. (Add the ability to offer one private placement sponsor, and your coverage of probable client needs will approach 95%.)

In the meantime, our best advice is:

DISCOVER ONE RELP
WHOSE STORY YOU ABSOLUTELY LOVE.
THEN . . .
SELL WHAT YOU LOVE,
NOT WHAT YOU MERELY "UNDERSTAND."

Now you have to go out and tell that story eight dozen times. Tell it to your spouse; tell it to your kids. Next time you pick up the dry cleaning, ask the owner if he'll listen to you for four minutes while you try to sell him something. Tell it to your golfing buddies (once on the front nine, once on the back nine and again at the 19th hole). Tell it to the maitre d' at your favorite restaurant. Tell it to your pastor (it's about time he had to listen to someone else talk for a while).

Make a game out of it. (Those six words are the very best advice you've ever gotten about *all* selling, by the way.) Just tell the story until you're so enthused, excited and happy that you just won't let a day go by without telling somebody else.

Everything will fall into place when you behave this way. The converse is also true: The chances of becoming an effective RELP communicator/salesperson in defiance of this rule are virtually nonexistent.

Most of us accepted long ago the eternal truth that, before we sell, we must be sold. That's all we are talking about here. Very often, the mere fact that you have tremendous enthusiasm for a particular RELP will be enough for many people to share your feelings and invest along with you. (Here's a very important principle: Own even a small piece of the RELP you're selling, and your effectiveness increases by a factor of three or more.)

When your prospect doesn't feel there's a fit between the RELP you love and his particular investment needs, an amazing thing happens. Most often, the client respects and even likes you for the genuine affection you have for your product, and he'll tell you, reasonably and without argument, why his needs differ. When you're offering a partnership that you really love, a prospect doesn't get mad at you. Instead, he declines the product *without rejecting you*. And, believe it or not, that's really the second best thing that can happen to you. (The best thing is, of course, having the prospect say, "Great! I love it! I'll buy it!")

When your product is rejected but your presentation is respected, you win because:

WHEN A PROSPECT TELLS YOU WHY YOUR RELP DOESN'T FIT, HE'S TOLD YOU WHAT HE'LL BUY.

This result is the ultimate reason why selling what you love always works. Your warmth and conviction have convinced the prospect that you're a worthwhile person with whom to do business. He doesn't throw you out when you show him the wrong RELP; he tells you what he needs. If you can simply understand him, or can convey to your home office what he's looking for, you're virtually assured of a sale on the next call — because then you'll be able to show him what he told you he wants to buy.

Isn't having the prospect tell you his needs infinitely better than agonizing endlessly over what particular RELP fits what particular need? Isn't that relationship much healthier, in the context of your agenda as a communicator/salesperson?

Product knowledge, as a precondition of your selling effort, will never get you where you want to be. Concentrate on what RELPs do, simplify, rely on experts (don't be one), and sell with personal conviction.

In light of all you've read, shouldn't this chapter have been entitled "What You *Don't* Need to Know?" Sure . . . but it was too early for that. You might have concluded that this book is anti-intellectual, hard-sell, or some other awful thing. Still, this chapter is essential to your appreciation of the whole book, and you'd be well advised to stop here, go back, and read it again.

SUMMARY

- Define what your clients can reasonably require of you.

- Set your own agenda.

- You will always be asked a question you can't answer, so stop worrying about it.

- Let your instinctive powers of simplification take over.

- RELPs aren't complex unless you make them complex.

- Communicate what a RELP does, not what a RELP is.

- Sell what you love, not what you just "understand."

- When a prospect tells you why your RELP doesn't fit, he's told you what he'll buy.

3

Some Basic, Comforting Real Estate Concepts

We've already suggested that the first step to mastering the RELP sales process is to rely on one fundamental investment concept, in order to keep the investor's attention focused on a higher (and genuinely more important) plane. And before we're through, you'll know how to do that, comfortably and convincingly, with every important RELP product type.

Your ability to become comfortable with basic real estate concepts, and to recall them in a wide variety of sales situations, will govern to a very great extent your ability to sell RELPs successfully. If, on the other hand, your instinct is to regard broad concepts as essential oversimplifications, or as a way of glossing over (or of drawing attention away from) more specific and more painful truths, you may already be in more trouble than we can hope to get you out of.

All the best communicators/salespeople operate on this assumption:

**BEFORE YOU CAN SELL,
YOU MUST BE SOLD.**

This chapter is intended to give you a basic understanding of real estate fundamentals, because we see so many potentially fine RELP salespeople banging their heads endlessly against walls of detail and never breaking through to the very real comfort that comes with an understanding of the basic business of real estate. Even the fact that real estate *is* a business, one that lends itself to readily understandable business analysis, seems to stun any number of otherwise very bright salespeople.

Let's put it another way: The tactics are never going to make any real sense to you, and you'll never be able to convince anyone else of how sensible they are, unless you first have a pretty accurate understanding of the strategy.

REAL ESTATE BEATS THE COMPETITION

Let's begin with the essential perception:

REAL ESTATE CONSISTENTLY OUTPERFORMS SECURITIES INVESTMENTS.

Actually, we already tried to plant this seed way back in the introduction to this book. Only there, we said simply, "Real estate is a superior investment in a wide variety of economic environments." We showed you a chart which suggested that real estate works well during both high and low inflation. But what that chart also shows is something even more profound. So let's take a look at it again (see the next page).

Now, do you see what the chart is *really* saying? **Real estate always outperforms stocks and bonds over any intermediate-term holding period.**

Well, of course it does. Real estate *has to,* or else nobody would ever buy it. Why? Because real estate isn't immediately liquid in the way that stocks and bonds are. And one of the oldest investment axioms in the world is that the less liquid an investment is, the more it has to yield. The investor requires more yield for accepting real estate's relative illiquidity.

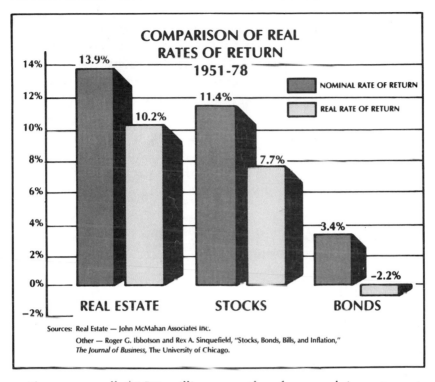

COMPARISON OF REAL
RATES OF RETURN
1951-78

NOMINAL RATE OF RETURN

REAL RATE OF RETURN

13.9%

10.2%

11.4%

7.7%

3.4%

-2.2%

REAL ESTATE   STOCKS   BONDS

Sources: Real Estate — John McMahan Associates Inc.
Other — Roger G. Ibbotson and Rex A. Sinquefield, "Stocks, Bonds, Bills, and Inflation,"
The Journal of Business, The University of Chicago.

You can sell $100-million worth of several investment-grade common stocks in an hour on the New York Stock Exchange, and nobody will ever know you've been there. The same selling program in government bonds probably couldn't take you much longer than ten minutes, and away you'd go.

But a building, or complex of buildings, worth $100 million could easily take you three to six months of careful and protracted negotiations to sell, unless you were just plain lucky.

You don't buy real estate with money you're likely to need in a big hurry, because you can't count on being able to liquidate the investment very quickly. Therefore, **you demand of real estate an appreciably higher return than you would earn in more liquid investments — and you get it.** Otherwise, nobody would play.

If you still can't see this instinctively, make believe you're the Equitable Life Assurance Society of the United States. Your whole mission in life is to pursue an investment strategy that lets you pay cash demands, cover your expenses, and have a reasonably competitive return left over. Your actuaries have told you exactly how many people are going to die, how many will let policies lapse, and how many will borrow out cash values over the next five years. Your marketing and investment people have projected cash inflows. So, you've got a very clear idea of what your cash position is going to be.

Why, then, would you ever go to the bother of being a major owner of real estate?

Simple. Because, first, you're only investing funds which your experts tell you you're not going to need soon. And second, you have the strong conviction that your real estate investments are going to significantly outperform stocks and bonds. Otherwise, you'd say "the heck with it" and just buy more securities.

Yield and liquidity always go in opposite directions. The more liquid an investment, the less the yield. The converse is also (and most importantly) true: The less liquid the investment (like real estate), the more the return; otherwise, professional investors will shy away. We can safely say that no one becomes a RELP superstar without perceiving this relationship.

The RELP superstar almost never hears the objection: "Yes, but real estate isn't liquid." Yet, on the rare occasions when he does hear it, he can say, with the utmost enthusiasm and conviction, "That's right. Real estate *isn't* very liquid. That's one reason it's so great. If real estate were liquid, the potential return wouldn't be *nearly* so high."

A corollary, one with which virtually all experienced securities salespeople are familiar, is that investors' perceptions of liquidity needs are rarely very accurate. And, with a little gentle probing, the *real* liquidity need is separable from the *perceived* liquidity need.

When an investor objects to real estate investments on the basis of illiquidity, he's really saying, "I'm afraid I may need my capital back at some point during the life of this investment, when I can't get at it." Later on, in the chapters on Q&A, we will develop the theory that an investor's *stated* objection is never his real objection. For the moment, please accept that the investor is not making an accurate statement of what he means. Reacting directly to what the investor says, rather than probing for what he really means, is always the wrong thing for the communicator/salesperson to do.

The operative word in this investor's statement of concern is, of course, "afraid." You can't, and wouldn't want to, take the illiquidity of real estate out of the equation because of the yield premium you get in return. So, what you have to do is overcome his fear. You have to ask him this question: "In the next five to seven years (the anticipated holding perod of the RELP you'd like him to own), what might happen to make you need this relatively small part of your capital (or net worth) in such a hurry?"

Investors generally don't have a very good answer to this question. Often, particularly for older investors, the liquidity issue is a euphemism for the fear of dying and leaving an illiquid investment in the estate. (Bond salesmen have run into this phenomenon forever. Our favorite story is about the bond salesman who called his 78-year-old client with a new-issue, ten-year bond. "Ten-year bonds?" says the client, "Why, I've even stopped buying green bananas!")

Much more often than not, an investor's estate has no pressing liquidity needs. On the rare occasion when you do find such a problem, suggest increasing his life insurance, help him sell off some of his other assets, or do both. (Remember: When a prospect tells you why your RELP doesn't fit, he's told you what he'll buy or, in this case, sell. In a situation like this, there is no such thing as "no sale.")

Incidentally, we are convinced that most of the prospects who have bowed you out on the issue of liquidity have, *within the week,* blithely strolled down to the local savings bank and socked the money into a 5-year CD. So much for perceptions of liquidity needs!

Another variation on this theme involves private placements. Here the prospect may look at a five-year schedule of capital contributions and say, "I don't want to be tied up that long." In this liquidity objection the prospect is saying that he's afraid his income level won't hold up during the pay-in period. The only approach here is to probe to see if there are realistic, dark clouds on the horizon, or if he is generalizing an anxiety about his career.

So, to sum up:

REAL ESTATE IS A WONDERFUL INVESTMENT IN WHICH YOU TRADE OFF SOME LIQUIDITY FOR A DEMONSTRABLY HIGHER RETURN.

At best, the relative illiquidity of real estate is one of its greatest selling points. At worst, an investor is using illiquidity as a smoke screen for anxieties which, when intelligently probed, always tell you more about your prospect and about his real financial and emotional needs.

HOW REAL ESTATE CYCLES WORK

People love to buy real estate, as you know, because their personal experience with real estate has been so good — their home is worth three times its original cost. But trying to reason directly from home ownership to a general understanding of real estate investments isn't going to work.

First of all, your house rose so much in value primarily because its *replacement cost* went up. Income-producing real estate doesn't appreciate just because replacement cost rises. A rise in value occurs if, and to the extent that, rents and cash flows from rents rise:

REAL ESTATE HAS CYCLES, LIKE ALL OTHER BUSINESSES, AND IS VALUED ON EARNINGS OR ANTICIPATED YIELD.

What a relief it is just to grab onto these two ideas and hold them for a while. When you begin to understand these concepts, you'll have greatly increased your ability to present the business logic of any particular RELP.

Real estate, indeed, is created (and later sells) for its yield. A real estate project starts when a developer and a lender see an opportunity to realize a superior return (yield) by manufacturing a certain kind of real estate product for a certain market. Let's say the product is office space, the market is North Dallas and the time is 1979. (Not that the details really matter, but they make the discussion less abstract and more easily comprehensible. What counts is the description of the real estate cycle based on anticipated yields.)

North Dallas is (in 1979) one of the fastest growing office markets in America. The growth of that booming, economically diversified city is being pulled north by a combination of cheap land, good roads, and the ever-present intangible called desirability. Interest rates are very high, which makes an increasing amount of proposed development in cities not experiencing such great demand fail to "pencil out" (that's when the probable cash flow of the developed property won't pay a decent return on the costs of construction). So even more development money gravitates toward the "sure," high-demand markets . . . like Big D.

And with excellent reason. Lots of factors argue for continued increases in cash flows for good new office construction: the ability to increase rents, the rate at which new space is being absorbed, population trends, job growth, low taxes, little or no organized labor.

At some point later in the cycle, the numbers become so well known to developers and lenders (who take increased comfort when so many other "smart" operators are building) that a real building boom is uncorked. (Or, as Jack Crozier of Murray Financial observed at the time, looking out from his office on Dallas' LBJ Freeway, "The state bird of Texas is the construction crane.")

Then, the rate of growth in the economy (which people like to extrapolate as far into the future as is necessary to make their deals work) starts to settle down somewhat; trees do not grow all the way to the sky. Slowly at first, but with increasing visibility, more office space becomes available than there are folks coming to town looking to rent. Vacancy rates increase; rent increases slow, then stop. Longer and longer rental concessions (free-rent periods) become commonplace. Finally, rents are cut and start coming down.

New construction stops. The popular press begins to pick up stories about the office market "glut." Lenders stampede out of town like sheep in a thunderstorm. The six o'clock news profiles a developer who's gone bankrupt, ending with a long shot of the bank's repossessor driving the developer's Rolls Royce away, or putting a padlock on his palatial mansion. Despair is everywhere, and everyone *knows* you'll lose your shirt investing in North Dallas office space. In other words, if you build, you not only won't earn a decent return, you may even lose your capital.

And then one day, a real estate broker calls the president of an insurance company in Chicago. "There's a brand-new, well constructed 200,000-square foot, empty, office building about to go back to the lender. You can lease the whole thing for $10 a foot, with tenant finishing free and no rent for six months on a five-year lease. And the lender, which desperately wants to avoid foreclosing, will give your company a nifty line of credit." The Chicago insurance man, paying $30 a foot where he is, never really cared that much for wind and snow to begin with. The appeal of lower rent (and probably lower labor cost, too) falling to the bottom line makes him say, "I'll take it."

A week later, the scene is repeated, and again two days later. Then, a Fortune 500 company announces that it's moving its headquarters to Dallas because the developers, the banks and the city itself have made an offer the company can't refuse.

Occupancies start nudging up. Rents are still stagnant, of course, and there's zero new construction. The lenders are too smart for Dallas; they are out in southern California helping to overbuild Irvine. Absorption is picking up. Some potential renters can't find the right space in the right location. Occupancy, one source says quietly, may hit 90% in Dallas by the end of the year.

And one day a developer ambles in off the street and says to his local banker, "You know, occupancy in North Dallas is getting awfully tight, and rents may be getting ready to step out smartly. There's tremendous job growth, with all the new companies moving to town. Maybe we ought to think about putting up a little office building . . . " And the cycle begins anew.

MANUFACTURING INCOME

One of the many things you can infer from the foregoing fable is that the construction cycle is the underlying phenomenon in real estate. In the short run, rents will rise and fall partly as a response to supply and demand for space in local markets. As rents rise and fall so does cash flow or return (yield) on investment. **All investment cycles are based on anticipated returns.** In other words, once you've accepted that investment-grade real estate trades as a function of its cash yield, you've implicitly accepted that rising rents (and cash flows) should carry values higher.

The correct conclusion to draw is that real estate is more similar to the other investments you're accustomed to than perhaps you thought it was. Years ago, Ira M. Koger, who invented the concept of the suburban office park, reluctantly allowed his company, Koger Properties, to go public. Almost from that day on, he was bedeviled by the fact that Wall Street and the stock market could never understand the real value in the company. The securities analysts chose to key on Koger Properties' relatively small earnings per share and failed to focus on the company's large and growing cash flow (which, thank heaven, translated into little taxable net income because of the substantial shelter of depreciation).

Finally, in a fit of ire and creativity, Ira Koger hit on a simple way of explaining, even to the green eyeshades of Wall Street, what his company did. He said:

REAL ESTATE IS
A MANUFACTURER OF RENT STREAMS.

That phrase says it all. Go beyond the mere physical details of what a particular property is (an apartment complex, an office building . . . who cares?), and see, instead, a box capable of producing an inflation-hedged income stream. Then realize that what the market will pay for that income is the real value of the box.

RENTS RISE WITH INFLATION

But, over the intermediate to longer term, here's another major comfort-builder:

RENTS ARE PRETTY CLOSELY
RELATED TO INFLATION.

Most potential RELP salespeople instinctively believe that real estate's income-producing capability is, broadly speaking, indexed to inflation. When the income rises along with inflation, so does the price (value) of your property over the long pull. They know, as well, that real estate is worth some acceptable multiple of earnings.

Well and good. The only trouble is that most potential RELP salespeople haven't really got their arms around how rents are related to inflation in the first place. You may eagerly, and instinctively, embrace the concept, but you aren't necessarily able to tell which is the chicken and which is the egg. That uncertainty is kind of anxiety-producing. Like the emperor with no clothes, one day you are going to run into an investor who doesn't realize what a dumb question this is, and he's going to ask:

*"But, **why** are rents tied to inflation?"*

And you are going to be stuck for the answer. So here's a nice, simplified explanation. And once again, you may be pleased to note just how many common investor questions it answers *comfortably* and *conceptually*. It's just an amplification of the description of the construction and development cycle, served up with a slightly different spin on the ball:

INFLATION IN BUILDING COSTS STRANGLES NEW CONSTRUCTION, UNLESS AND UNTIL RENTS RISE ENOUGH TO JUSTIFY THE HIGHER COSTS.

(This is alternatively known as the Brother-In-Law Theorem of Rents, because it is so simple that even your brother-in-law can comprehend it.)

It isn't material whether the inflation in building costs comes from: (1) higher interest rates; or (2) increased costs of land, bricks and sticks; or (3) all of the above. Anything that pushes up the cost of new construction, without the prospect of higher rents to offset increased costs, stops new construction (restricts supply). This relationship should be evident to anybody who can add and do a bit of long division. (Admittedly, that qualification excludes many lenders, which is why real estate cycles tend to be exaggerated at the tops and the bottoms.)

Go back to North Dallas office space (or, if you're getting bored with that, make it Memphis garden apartments — it matters not). When we left our story, building was about to start up again. Although occupancy had tightened up considerably, rents were still pretty depressed. Our heroes (the developer and his banker) haven't built anything in a couple of years, so they have to go out and determine costs. They discover some disturbing news when they re-price construction.

First of all, the price of land hasn't gone down. With the trough of the cycle well past, prices for good land have actually taken a nice bounce. Next, they look at prices for bricks and sticks. Sure enough, even though the producer price index may have only crept up about 4% in each of the last two years, construction materials now cost 10%–12% more than a few years ago.

How about labor? No help there, either. With unemployment at its low point for the past decade, wages are going north. When you factor in the increased costs of benefits (health care costs are clipping ahead in double digits), that piece of the puzzle looks very pricey. Interest rates are the only place our boys have gotten any kind of a break.

At the end of the day, when our developer and his friendly banker put all the numbers in the calculator, the news isn't good. Barring some very smart rise in rents, new construction costs too much to make sense. So, the inevitable happens: Population and job growth continue, absorption goes on ticking up, vacancy rates shrink, and then rents start to rise. With expanding demand and no new supply coming on stream, rents keep rising until . . . they justify new construction. It was ever thus. And there isn't much sense holding your breath until the cycle works any other way, because it won't.

Only real estate offers you the reasonable assurance that its income, and therefore its value in the marketplace, are going to be drawn forward by inflation. And now you know *exactly* why you want your clients to invest in real estate.

Common stocks won't do that for you. High inflation always means high interest rates, and high interest rates just murder the stock market. Precious metals don't work, either. Metal prices may rise when capital flees out of currencies, which it does in inflationary times. But, metals not only don't produce income, they cost money to store and insure.

And, heaven knows, bonds are a disaster. Inflation drains away the real purchasing power of a bond's income stream while you're holding it, and debases the purchasing power of the currency you are paid back when your bond matures.

There is just one danger to the communicator/salesperson in the analysis you've just read: **Don't conclude that you have to have inflation to make money in real estate.** That's never been true (remember the performance table at the beginning of this chapter), and it's not true today.

Why? Because whenever you get a prolonged period of low inflation, interest rates go way down. Low interest rates translate into good news for real estate, in two powerful ways.

First, mortgage borrowing costs go down, which means more cash flow even if rents stay where they are. And more cash flow, of course, always means more value.

Second, though this is more subtle and less obvious, a long period of lower interest rates can result in lower "cap rates" and higher values for real estate. In other words, if the yields we demand from corporate bonds, Treasury securities, utility stocks, etc., are going lower, so are the yields we demand of real estate. Just like a bond, if you buy real estate at a lower current yield, you are paying a higher price.

One virtue of real estate as an investment is that it experiences less volatility in the market range of current yields than fixed income securities. As a broad gauge, the current yield of real estate fluctuates between 8% and 10%. While the price movement is much narrower for real estate than for bonds, declining interest rates can boost real estate prices somewhat.

SURE CURES

If you're finding yourself growing to love the notion of a reliable real estate cycle, here's another concept that not only follows logically, but also offers a great deal of emotional comfort:

TIME AND MONEY CURE ALL ILLS IN REAL ESTATE.

Nothing can absolutely insulate you from making an investment at the wrong point in the real estate cycle, or from misjudging just where in the cycle you really are. And even when you buy a perfectly good property in a perfectly healthy market, nothing can save you from having the industry come in behind you and completely overbuild the market.

So what can you do? The answer is, of course, ride out the cycle. If you really do believe in the cycle, then you've already accepted the notion that, *in time,* when new construction stops, occupancies and then rents will head up again as the inexorable demographics take over.

But that's only one part of the equation. You have to have the money — either in reserve within the partnership, or in the strength of the general partner — to cover cash shortfalls and maintain the property in competitive condition during a period of low occupancies and rents. That's where the general partner really earns his fees: in the crunch. (One of the interesting things to do, as you're working your way up the RELP learning curve, is to ask the sponsor's representatives to tell you about some of their problem properties: what went wrong, and what they're doing to work through the difficulties.)

The main point: As long as you accept the inevitability of the cycle, time and money (and a lot of commitment) will see you through. To salespeople and prospects alike, that notion ought to be mighty reassuring.

CASH FLOW CAN OUTPACE RENTS

In the previous discussions, rents and cash flow were treated as pretty much the same. However, cash flow can actually increase *faster* than rents if you finance property with mortgages (this is referred to as using leverage). While rents and operating expenses may be increasing at the same rate, cash flow may, in fact, be expanding at a greater rate. That's because debt service is usually a fixed amount (think of the amount you pay on your home mortgage). Debt service on the mortgage for income-producing real estate may run 65% or 70% of total costs.

When rents are escalating, the gross income of the property is rising. But, the variable *operating* expenses comprise a very distinct minority of the total expenses, usually 35% or less. If you've ever heard a presentation of an all-cash RELP or mini-warehouse fund, you'll immediately see the point. The sponsor claims to break even at 28%-30% occupancy. What he's saying is that operating expenses are 30% or less of gross rents.

One of the great conceptual benefits of leveraged real estate, then, is:

**RENT INCREASES FLOW MAINLY
TO THE BOTTOM LINE
BECAUSE EXPENSES ARE PREDOMINANTLY FIXED.**

While you're getting a stronger feel for some basic real estate relationships, remember that real estate investment gives you a unique opportunity:

OWNERSHIP OF REAL ESTATE LETS YOU DEPRECIATE AN APPRECIATING ASSET.

Perhaps these days such a commonplace notion is taken for granted. But some of the superior return potential of real estate comes from this source. After all, during a period when a real estate investment isn't producing cash flow, depreciation will provide you with tax losses which will shelter future income from taxes. When your real estate venture is providing cash flow, depreciation can shelter some of the cash flow from taxation, thereby increasing your after-tax return.

All the while, what you're really doing is enjoying the act of accounting for the supposedly *declining* value of an asset which is, in reality, steadily *rising* in value.

Compare the ability to recover capital free of tax in real estate (through depreciation) with other investments you know, and you'll see again why, in the race to provide superior returns, real estate is a winner.

(It may also help you take some of the mystery out of the question of where tax losses come from to note that virtually all "artificial," meaning noncash, real estate tax deductions are produced by depreciation. All other deductions, like mortgage interest or deductible fees, are just business expenses, deductible in real estate or widget manufacturing.)

SELL, DON'T ANALYZE

Chapter 2 concluded, as one of its main messages, that real estate limited partnerships are not particularly complex. Chapter 3 has been devoted to promoting an understanding that the real estate business itself is not mysterious.

Explaining these fundamentals is as analytical as we'll ever get in these pages. This discussion wasn't meant to give you a rigorous education in real estate; such an effort is beyond the scope of this book. The purpose is to carry through on everything you've read so far, and to confirm to you that the weight of anxiety you may bring to the selling of RELPs is (a) unfounded in business reality and (b) destructive of any real hope for success in selling these fascinating investments.

This book isn't really meant to build your factual knowledge of RELPs. That's no fun — and besides, it's done better in so many other places. Read Bob Stanger's *How to Evaluate Real Estate Partnerships* if you thirst for knowledge and analytical power. Read *The Stanger Report* every month (and don't put it down 'til you understand it) if you want to follow structural and financing trends in the RELP industry.

If you can't see your way clear to becoming an effective communicator/salesperson of RELPs, it's going to be because of blocks you've set up in your own psychology. But nothing intrinsic to RELPs or to the real estate business should cement those blocks.

Grab hold of the wholesaler for the RELP you think you're falling in love with, and/or the internal wholesaler for your firm, and tell them: "Look, I'm determined to become a superstar in your product. *My* job is to keep working on selling until I succeed. *Your* job is to live with me, talk to me, make calls with me, answer a million dumb questions for me, and generally show as much tenacity as I do (not more, but certainly not less) until I finally break through, *no matter how long that takes.*"

We'll talk later on about how to use staff people systematically. All we're trying to do here is tell you where you should be looking for the product knowledge you need, and give you the attitude you need to look for it successfully.

Now, enough about all this factual stuff. No more practicing your snowplow turns on the bunny slopes. Get your skis on, and let's go hit the mountain.

SUMMARY

- This chapter was for you, because before you can sell, you must be sold.

- Real estate consistently outperforms all other classes of securities. It has to, because it isn't liquid.

- Real estate, like all other businesses, runs in cycles based on its anticipated yield.

- Real estate trades at a multiple of its income.

- Rents in the short run are closely related to supply and demand.

- Rents in the long run are closely related to inflation because:
  - (a) Inflation strangles new construction unless and until rents rise enough to justify the higher costs, so
  - (b) Even in low-inflation periods, real estate becomes more valuable, as mortgages are refinanced at lower rates, and/or as "cap rates" go down.

- Real estate really does hedge against inflation in a way no other income-producing asset can.

- With leveraged real estate most expenses are fixed, so cash flow can actually increase faster than rents.

- Time and money cure all ills in real estate.

- Ownership of real estate lets you depreciate an appreciating asset.

- Stop analyzing. Start selling.

4

Prospecting I: Establishing a Plan

The salesperson starting out to become a RELP superstar has three basic decisions to make:

(1) how to prospect;
(2) who to prospect; and
(3) what to prospect with.

Actually, the third category is the most important, because your answers to the first two will flow from your answer to the third. The question of what to prospect with, in turn, is really an inquiry into:

(1) who you are;
(2) what your natural market is; and
(3) what you love to sell.

To a remarkable degree, after you have been in investment sales for any length of time, you end up with a book of accounts who are very much like you. Your clients may not be the same age or sex, or have the same marital status, income, net worth and investment goals. But they tend to be people who *think* the way you do, and who like your approach to solving problems and choosing investments. This observation must be true, or your clients probably wouldn't go on doing business with you.

So, look at just what you love to sell, and what kind of people you love to sell to. Sit down, go through your book of accounts (the essence of your natural market), and see what you've been most successfully selling over the last year or so.

- Is the common denominator safety and income? Great. You've learned some major truths about people, about wealth, and about yourself. The great bulk of most people's net worth, you've discovered, isn't make-a-killing money. It's *don't-get-killed* money. This kind of capital simply seeks preservation and a "decent" return (although definitions of those terms vary all over the lot, of course). You like to work with don't-get-killed money because the goal strikes a strong, responsive chord in you. You don't much like sticking your neck out. Like your clients, you prefer to sleep nights.

  Still, your experience with bonds, CDs, or even stocks that trade on dividend yield has left something to be desired. You've been around long enough to realize that capital preservation has a hollow ring if the principal amount is losing ground to inflation, failing to hold the purchasing power of the dollar.

  At the time of writing this book, the environment for debt securities is sort of schizophrenic. To wit, interest rates have been working lower and lower throughout the 1980s, which means bond prices in your clients' portfolios are rising. But, as bonds and CDs mature, the income producing capacity of the capital is less. And investors are only human: Whether they need, or are just used to, higher levels of income from "safe" investments, the normal tendency is always to reach, somehow, to maintain income in declining interest rate markets.

  But, there are only two ways to do that, and both of them are terribly dangerous. One is to come down in investment quality, the perils of which are self-evident. The other may be even more risky: reaching for yield by lengthening maturities. Why is this perilous? In a period of rising interest rates, nothing gets mauled like bonds. And the longer the maturity, the worse the damage.

Are you at all inclined to think that interest rates, like all economic phenomena, tend to run in cycles? If so, could we currently be an awful lot closer to cyclical interest rate lows than to the highs? Then, investors' willingness to stretch out maturities for current yield has to scare you to death. (Maybe you think a meaningful upturn in rates is as much as a couple of years away. But if the folks are loading up on ten and fifteen-year paper, the bond market may not eat their lunch, but by dinner time the situation could be kind of grim.)

You are a natural to begin a prospecting program right in your own account book, the goal of which is to expose people to a reasonably high level of current income and a whole lot of protection against higher rates of interest or inflation. You should direct yourself, with a rationale and a conviction, to participating mortgage RELPs and/or low-leverage equity RELPs.

Are you getting the idea? Approach the product selection question from the direction of who you are, what your clients need and what your hopes and fears for your clients are. The *conceptual* answer of what type of RELP to show your accounts will jump right off the page at you. There may be two dozen RELPs on your firm's calendar of approved deals. If you start from the viewpoint that you have to learn to compare and contrast them, you'll never be seen or heard from again.

- All right, suppose you see your mission differently. You want to make your clients' capital grow. You think capital is just like personality: If it's not growing, it's dying. But, you're finding that, even after a couple of years of steadily (and, here and there, even spectacularly) rising stock prices, people just aren't willing to expose enough of their capital to equity markets. And dealing in stocks, clients are apt to use a discount broker or negotiate your commission down to the point where you don't make a decent buck for your effort. (The painful issue of your compensation has to be allowed to surface somewhere in this discussion, after all.)

Well, then, what *will* they buy that gives them the potential for meaningful growth of capital? You guessed it: leveraged-equity real estate. Once again, you know *conceptually* where in the RELP calendar you will find your favorite RELP.

- Now, suppose you're a different breed of cat entirely. You're kind of intrigued with private placements. First of all, the sort of people who can buy privates are your clients and the people you are prospecting. You have arrived at the full realization of a basic career relationship between you and your marketplace: **The income of a securities salesperson is an absolute function of the income of his clients.** So, you have a tremendous incentive to go after the big hitters.

And now, after tax reform and the death of the concept of "tax shelter," private placements are undergoing a metamorphosis. They're turning into vehicles that can deliver very high levels of tax-sheltered income.

So what you're looking at now is an investment medium that's going to be phenomenally attractive to the wealthy investor who typically buys municipal bonds in $50,000 to $100,000 lots.

As a potential private placement superstar, that's got to make you feel great. Because your instincts tell you, quite correctly, that:

**THE MARKET FOR TAX-FREE INCOME
EXCEEDS THE MARKET FOR "TAX SHELTER"
BY A FACTOR OF INFINITY.**

If this approach to RELP sales grabs you, you have just

eliminated 90% of the product (as well as the prospecting techniques you hear in sales meetings) and can zero in on private placements as the right direction for your natural attitudes and aptitudes.

In other words you already have an instinctively correct idea as to what kinds of people you should be prospecting and what kinds of RELPs you should be prospecting with. Stop worrying about the bewildering variety of RELPs that are out there, and start concentrating on the facts that:

YOU HAVE TO BE WHO YOU ARE, AND YOU HAVE TO SELL WHAT YOU LOVE.

As your knowledge of real estate grows, so will your appreciation of how many kinds of real estate solutions there are for a wide variety of client needs. But, knowledge comes with time. What's at issue now is how and where you begin. **RELP sales success must start with action, not knowledge.**

HOW TO PROSPECT

When you begin consciously working to alter the composition and character of your business, what you're really doing is working to change yourself. That's something to really think about when you start any major new prospecting program. There is a *very finite limit* to how much change you can effect in a short time. Trying to accomplish too much too quickly is just a subtle form of self-sabotage.

Yet, highly motivated salespeople who determine to make a major new step in their business, such as mastering RELP sales skills, very often try to do too much at once. Two obvious pitfalls pop up. Some salespeople say, "I'm going to make a whole lot of RELP presentations and do a whole lot of business." Here the goal is so vague that it can't be measured, and so it just withers away under the pressure of rejection and unanswered questions.

The other pitfall is even worse: setting a series of goals that are not sustainable for any length of time. Suppose you now try to make a RELP presentation perhaps four or five times a month. You clap this book closed when you finish reading it and say, "From now on, I'm going to make ten RELP presentations a day. If I close just one out of ten, and average $10,000 per ticket, I'll be doing $200,000 a month."

Completely doomed! **You're trying to effect too much change too quickly,** and you're exposing yourself to the pain that comes with a lot of rejection you're not used to, and a lot of questions you can't answer.

Not only that, you've defined your goals in the wrong terms. All of us tend to define success in terms of closed sales. When sales don't come at the forecast rate, we have even more impetus to write off the prospecting program as a failure.

Forget closing sales for a while. Try to see what the point of a RELP prospecting program is. First and foremost:

THE GOAL IS TO BE ABLE TO MAKE RELP PRESENTATIONS.

In the process you will begin to catalog the general run of questions you'll be asked, and to learn the answers to them. As you do, **the sales will follow automatically.**

Your objective, therefore, should just be to create a prospecting program that you can comfortably follow without disrupting the conduct of your present business. And **the reward you look for should simply be the act of completing your prospecting schedule.** In other words, let your goal be accomplishing a set number of presentations each and every day, even if you:

MAKE ONE PRESENTATION PER DAY.

Behavior is only successfully modified by rewarding the act of trying to change, as Dr. Aaron Hemsley says in his brilliant program, "The Psychology of Maximum Sales Production." That's why the coach gives somebody who makes a great tackle, or catches a great pass, a sticker for his football helmet, whether the team wins the game or not. He's reinforcing the behavior that *leads* to success.

So the first thing you have to do is establish that you'll do something of a RELP prospecting nature every day, *even if it's just to make one call.*

Odd as it may seem, this goal is very different from determining that you'll make five calls per week. With a weekly goal, you can skip several days and, after having built up a lot of anxiety about it, try to pack all five calls into the last day. (Conversely, you might try to do them all on Monday, so you could go a whole week without having to make calls.) It won't work. Some activity every day is critical to establishing an effective prospecting program.

When you can consistently make one presentation a day (or two, or three, or whatever number you pick as your minimum daily activity) for a whole month, you've established your "baseline." If you can't sustain that number each day, drop one call and try again. If that still won't work, drop back one more. Keep doing this until you find a set number of calls you can make every day for a month. When you've found your baseline level where you're functioning comfortably — where neither questions, nor objections, nor rejection can cause you to drop your program — you may be able to expand your prospecting ever so slightly. So add one call a day, and see if you can keep operating for a month at that new level.

If that expansion proves unsustainable, *for whatever reason,* stop. Go back to your baseline number, the last level of prospecting activity you could sustain. Prospect at the baseline for another month. Then, try adding one presentation a day again, and see if it will stick this time.

Pay no attention to your sales results — it's far too early for that. **Your goal must be to create the pattern of behavior which leads to RELP sales success,** and nothing more. And that pattern of behavior is simply to build up gradually, without disturbing the pattern of your other business, the number of RELP sales presentations you can make.

All great salespeople know that, in the end, who they spoke to, or even what they said, doesn't matter. They know, instead, that what matters is how many calls they make, because **the first and last truth about prospecting is that the numbers always work.** And, no matter how long it takes, the act of *slowly* building up the number of RELP calls you can make will be the final determinant of whether you ever emerge as a RELP superstar.

If you noodle with this concept a little longer, you'll arrive at the vital conclusion that:

NO SINGLE CALL MATTERS.

If you've placed your faith in the numbers, then go ahead and grind out the numbers (trying, if possible, to learn a little something from each call). The great benefit of that mind-set is that it lets you stop caring about any individual call, because you have made a (numbers) game out of prospecting. Just treat each presentation as an end in itself, as part of compiling your daily baseline number of RELP presentations.

The most amazing result of this way of thinking is that, when you stop worrying about each call, you immediately become more effective, simply because you're relaxed. Relaxation, of course, comes through to the client as confidence. And RELPs, as we've agreed, are the ultimate "confidence" sale.

What's even more important is that when you're relaxed, you're more creative. You think more quickly and clearly, and you're better able to handle questions and objections smoothly and give interesting answers. Everything else in this book lumped together won't help you achieve that confident and relaxed state until you accept, and put into practice, the fact that, as in all selling:

RELP PROSPECTING IS A NUMBERS GAME.

All success and all knowledge in RELPs is cumulative. And if we're right that you only learn by doing, the gradual development of a sustained, consistent pattern of calls is now the only thing that matters.

IRAs: THE RELP SALESPERSON'S "BOOT CAMP"

Suppose you accept the validity of establishing a daily prospecting regimen, but you genuinely have no idea what type of RELP is best suited to your style. Or perhaps you do know, but you're afraid to "experiment" on your clients. Where then do you begin?

Go the IRA route. Every investor has an IRA (most people still have the funds in a bank!) — or should have one — and many people have Keoghs or 401(k)s. Since retirement accounts are, by definition, long-term investments, real estate is a terrific strategic idea for inclusion in a retirement portfolio. The investment characteristics of real estate exactly match the investment objectives of a retirement fund. Real estate will provide growing income and principal value and will keep up with inflation.

But most important, you can talk to everyone you meet about IRA investment in real estate without agonizing over suitability. It's easy to make, as was suggested earlier, a goal-oriented game out of prospecting IRAs.

You can simply say, "I'm going to make two IRA presentations a day in the next month and just see what happens." What you're trying to do, of course, is talk yourself into making a fairly large number of relatively anxiety-free presentations, *the outcome of which you don't care that much about.* The advantages are that you quickly and painlessly accumulate a great deal of presentation experience, as well as an easy familiarity with the half-dozen or so questions people commonly ask about RELPs.

Now, find out what RELP products your firm suggests for IRAs. Pick one you can learn to love, and **buy the RELP for your own IRA.** It's worth repeating: Owning even a little of the RELP you're selling increases your effectiveness 300%.

The best time to prospect for IRA business is anytime *except* the sixty days before April 15th. Yes, everybody puts off funding his IRA until the last minute. So, if you wait until the period before April 15th, you've got time pressure working for you. But, the problem is everybody else is beating the bushes for IRA business then. The noise and confusion levels are too high. Joe DiMaggio and Bob Hope are doing TV commercials for bank IRAs, and the newspapers are crammed with full-page ads for CDs (" . . . which, if they compound at this rate until you're 65, will give you a retirement nest egg of *one million dollars!*"). The financial product salesman your client hasn't heard from in years is on the phone. The competition is awesome and the amount of time you'll waste comparing and justifying investment choices for IRAs is beyond belief.

Forget it. Try August, or some other time when nothing much is happening. End every conversation at the beach, the golf club, or the tennis court with, "Oh, by the way, have you made this year's contribution to your IRA account yet?" You're reasonably assured of nearly a 100% incidence of people saying, "No. I don't have to do that until next April." Then you can say, "Do you have income-producing real estate in your IRA portfolio yet?" In the overwhelming majority of cases the prospect will say he doesn't. All you have to say is, "Well, I think *every* retirement fund should own some real estate, if only for diversification and as an inflation hedge. The one *I'm buying* (or, if that isn't true, "the one *I'm recommending*") is . . . " Make a two-minute presentation of your favorite all-cash or participating mortgage RELP. (We'll show you exactly how to do that in Chapters 11 and 12.) Finish up with, "Would you like to read something about this kind of investment for your IRA?" That's all you have to do.

When you call the prospect back, ask immediately if he wants to go ahead and make the investment. (One of the great mistakes salespeople make is that they fail to try to close the way the Boston Irish used to vote — early and often.) If he isn't able to commit immediately, you'll hear a question or an objection. One of the great benefits of owning the RELP in your own IRA is that you can say, "You know, I thought about that when I was looking at the partnership for my own account, and I decided . . . ," and you go on to overcome the objection.

A major benefit of this process is that you very quickly get to see how few questions people will ask you about any RELP (and how frequently they recur). You take a lot of "Q&A anxiety" out of your psychology, which is a terrific confidence-builder. Sitting there cringing and thinking, "Uh oh, now he's going to ask me a question I can't answer," is the same as standing on a tennis court saying, "Uh oh, now he's going to hit a shot I can't get to." The thought becomes a self-fulfilling prophecy.

Please understand that the IRA route isn't recommended here as a major revenue-producing breakthrough to the exciting life of the RELP superstar. Far from it. The IRA is the lowest common denominator, the entry-level introduction to selling RELPs. If your anxiety levels are high about starting to prospect systematically with RELPs, the IRA approach will help. If you can't even bring yourself to do that, or some variation of it, there's probably no hope: Your difficulties may just be too overwhelming to be solved by anything in this book.

PROSPECTING FOR NEW ACCOUNTS WITH RELPS: TAKE IT REAL EASY

If you're just getting started, you may encounter some serious difficulties in soliciting new accounts using a RELP as your prospecting tool.

First, the RELP sale tends to be very relationship-oriented, and the RELP sales process, as we've established, is very much rooted in trust. Therefore, the degree of difficulty is relatively high in trying to do a lot of RELP business with people you're just approaching. That's not to say it can't or shouldn't be done — we are just trying to define the issues here.

A RELP isn't like a life insurance policy in which the client is looking to the insurance company for performance of a very clearly stated contract. With life insurance, your client doesn't feel he needs you for continuing guidance, or for interpretation of how his policy is doing. Or, think of the client who bought a stock from you. It may have been your idea, but he knows he can quote the stock (independently of you) every day, follow the company in any number of ways that don't necessarily involve you, and, finally, he can be out of the investment, anytime he likes, with a thirty-second phone call.

So these **traditional investments demand a very much lower "threshold of acceptance" of the salesperson by the client** than RELPs do. Since the client never fully understands a RELP in the way he thinks he understands traditional investments, his confidence in you is a much greater issue with RELPs. Since confidence and trust usually come only with time and favorable experience, RELPs are a relatively tough way to try to get to first base.

(Of course, in the financial planning approach, confidence and trust are established by gaining the prospect's acceptance of The Plan. Here, a RELP sale (or sales) may well occur in the first round of repositioning a client's assets. But that's beside the point. The planner isn't prospecting for new accounts with RELPs. He is prospecting with The Plan.)

The real danger of prospecting for new accounts with RELPs isn't the "degree of difficulty" factor but the resulting *rejection*. The emerging RELP superstar is going to have enough difficulty mastering a new product line without the anxiety of having 99 out of 100 prospects hang up on him.

Think about it. Say the best new-issue municipal bond you've seen in years is being offered, and you decide to make 500 cold calls in a week with it. Look what you have going for you:

- You completly understand the product.
- You can tell the story inside a minute.
- Everybody you talk to will instantly know what you're talking about.
- You know you'll talk to a lot of people who've bought municipal bonds before.
- You're an old hand at cold calling; therefore, rejection doesn't bother you much because you know the law of large numbers will *always* get you some accounts, which you can open over the phone.
- You're relaxed; therefore, you're effective.

Now hypothesize that you're prospecting new accounts with a RELP (a game at which you're fairly new). The product takes a relatively long time to explain. You can't quote yields or maturity dates. People don't seem to know what you're talking about. You haven't yet spoken to anybody who's ever bought a RELP before. You start internalizing the rejection. "The fact that all these people are turning me down is *my fault*. If only I *knew* more . . . I'm in so much pain . . . I can't stand it . . . I think I'll kill myself'' (or just go back to trading the Data General August 40s, which is the same thing, only slower). And you abort your prospecting program.

For a communicator/salesperson, a prospecting program is like a diet. You really ought to be on one for the rest of your career. Unfortunately, people tend to work on both prospecting and diets really hard for a very short time. You secretly hope to accomplish a lot, and then go back to the way you were living before. That's why the real secret of a RELP prospecting program is putting in a very gradual, relatively anxiety-free, consistent effort every day, knowing that significant results will occur over a long period of time. Cold-prospecting with RELPs is a hard road that's generally not conducive to establishing new accounts rapidly.

RED FLAGS IN THE SUNSET:
POPULAR PROSPECTING IDEAS THAT NEVER WORK

Let's spend a few minutes on some tactics, ideas and attitudes that are generally fatal to RELP sales success. In other words, here's how *not* to prospect.

(1) **MAILERS** — A very attractive, very seductive way to avoid the real work of prospecting is using mailers. Don't do it! The reason is that **a prospect does not know what he's being asked to buy** when he gets a glossy, beautifully photographed RELP mailing piece. If you send out mailers about municipal bonds or about annuities, you can have some confidence that a person who returns a card has a conceptual frame of reference for the investment being offered. Whether he's ever going to buy from you is another matter. But, at least you have some sense that he knows what you are selling.

RELP mailers simply don't offer that assurance of recognition of the investment. And the prettier and glossier the mailer is, the greater will be the response from people who wouldn't buy a RELP at gunpoint, but who just are subliminally turned on by the graphics.

But be invited, and even encouraged, to send out a very few mailers every day if you're going to follow each one up with a phone call as part of your baseline prospecting program.

(2) **ADVERTISING** — No matter how misleading you'll find the response to mailers, advertising is at least ten times worse.

You can manage the ineffectiveness of mailers, at least, by sending them to carefully selected, demographically upscale zip codes. That way you'll know your mailer will be thrown away with the Hammacher Schlemmer and Sharper Image catalogs. In other words, it will go out with a nice class of garbage.

But nothing can ever really prepare you for the thrill of getting back an advertising coupon filled out in purple crayon, or one neatly typed out with the return address of the maximum-security cell block at a nearby Federal penitentiary.

(3) **BOUGHT "TAX SHELTER" LEADS** — At least two big negatives are apparent in lists of tax shelter buyers. First, these lists are the most woefully overworked leads anywhere in creation. After all, what is the logic of these lists? They show you people who've made *five* (count 'em) limited partnership investments in the last two years! This is a great lead? Sounds more like a client who's wired into a source of RELPs he's totally content with.

The fact that the people on the lists have bought a lot of these investments usually means they've got a solid relationship with another salesperson. Do you really think you can break into that relationship with a cold call, or worse, a prospecting letter? If you do, somebody had better break it to you about the Tooth Fairy.

If you want to do some cold prospecting and are looking for lists, be a little creative. Seek out trade and professional directories. Ask your clients which ones *they* are listed in. Go to the major public libraries or large business school libraries, which accumulate directories in great abundance. This class of lead is an awful lot different from names on a bought list, which somebody bought the day before you did, and which somebody else will buy the day after.

Five minutes in the Brooklyn Business Library turned up these directories, all of which have addresses and phone numbers:

Leaders in Electronics
The Blue Book of Optometrists
International Robotics Industry Directory
Who's Who in Fashion
Directory of Iron and Steel Works (U.S. and Canada)
Who's Who in Engineering
National Directory of Minority and Woman-Owned
    Businesses.

The last one, by the way, is 1,600 pages long — so much for traditional notions about where leads are to be found.

One last thing about lists: The salesperson who still believes in "good lists" and "bad lists" doesn't really believe that RELP sales are a numbers game, and will therefore never succeed. The notion that talking to a few "good" leads will let you avoid the strain and frustration of talking to a lot of "bad" leads is simply an avoidance technique. It's a complicated way of saying, "I can't stand to make a lot of calls."

The idea that who you're talking to is important robs you of all the effortless spontaneity that comes from not caring. And that, of course, is why we told you to start slowly and gradually, then build the number of calls as your anxiety level about RELPs goes down and your confidence level edges up.

(4) **HOT DEALS** — Don't think you can build a RELP business on "hot deals." A systematic RELP prospecting program requires you to select a RELP that's going to be around

long enough for you to work on it seriously. Remember: The first thing you're trying to establish is an easy, comfortable, consistently sustainable prospecting program.

RELP prospecting with a red-hot, one-of-a-kind deal that's on allocation defeats your purpose. Oh, you may find it easy to get people excited about the RELP, and you may, in spite of yourself, make a couple of quick sales. But when the offering is over, you'll have learned nothing. And you may even manage to tick off some of your best prospects: the ones who don't move fast enough, and get shut out after you pump them up about the deal.

Your objective is to work systematically up the learning curve and arrive at the point where you'll be a RELP superstar *throughout the entire remainder of your career.* There is no quick fix. There is no Santa Claus. The only way to get elected is to go out there and shake hands with a lot of voters.

SUMMARY

- You have to be who you are and sell what you love. Approach the job of RELP prospecting by first working in your natural market.

- Start slowly. Make the same number of RELP presentations every day, even if that number is one.

- Your immediate object is not sales, but a sustained, and slowly building, number of calls. All your experience will be cumulative.

- RELP prospecting is a numbers game.

- IRA prospecting can be the RELP salesperson's boot camp, by letting you make a lot of low-anxiety presentations.

- Be sure you buy the RELP you want to sell for your own account.

- Cold prospecting with RELPs, when you're just starting out, may be injurious to your mental health, which may cause you to abort your prospecting program.

- Mailers, advertising and bought "tax shelter" leads are death.

- There are a lot of interesting lists around, if you look.

- There are no good leads or bad leads — only "the numbers."

- Don't RELP prospect with a "hot deal."

5

Prospecting II: Leveraging Up

Establishing a consistent, slowly building, daily prospecting program is the single most difficult — and, of course, most important — accomplishment you have to achieve. But once you have a program taking shape, you can begin raising your sights above the issue of making daily calls. You can start thinking about "leveraging" off the many resources available to you. And you can also begin to refine your approaches in a number of productive ways. These next steps are what this chapter is about.

One of the most beguiling attractions about RELPs is the extraordinary amount of help you can get (both within your firm and from the sponsors) in mastering the art of selling them really well. We want to look at three strategies in particular:

(1) the "wholesaler";
(2) networking; and
(3) seminars.

USE THE "WHOLESALER"

Once you identify a RELP (or, at the very least, a RELP type) that you can love and that fits your natural market, the first thing you ought to do is call for help. Step One in a successful prospecting program is enlisting the aid of the internal wholesaler who covers your office, as well as the RELP wholesaler.

The incredible truth is that most would-be RELP salespeople don't use the staff help that's available to them nearly enough. That is only natural because your essential decency may make you think: "Gee, I've never done a lot of business for these guys, and they're probably out there running around closing cases for big hitters, and they haven't got time for me, anyway."

Nuts! The big hitters are closing their own cases. The wholesaler is wandering from desk to desk in the Ames, Iowa office, watching an endless succession of producers' eyes glazing over as he vainly tries to interest them in his RELP. And he's praying: "Please, Lord, let me find just *one* salesperson today who's seriously, excitedly interested in learning to sell my RELP. I don't care if he couldn't spell "real estate" if you spotted him the r, both t's, and all the vowels; just give me somebody who *wants to work the product,* and I'll take it from there."

When Senator Bill Bradley was playing basketball for Princeton, his credo was something he'd picked up from "Easy" Ed Macauley. It said, "When you are not practicing, remember, someone somewhere *is* practicing, and when you meet him, he will win." Your attitude toward wholesalers should be just the same: When you are not using them, someone else is. And, at the same time you are trying and failing to make a sale without the wholesaler, the producer who's using him is closing a sale.

A book like this can (and will) give you a lot of general guidelines about how to prospect with RELPs, as well as how not to. But if you subscribe to the essential thesis that your first move has to be to take one RELP that you really love and tell that story 100 times, then it's crazy not to enlist the wholesaler's help.

Learning to sell RELPs takes enough work without your trying to reinvent the wheel. **Wholesalers are leverage because they know the answers to all the questions and objections in their sleep.** You need all the leverage you can get. Wholesalers can help you refine and sharpen your presentation. They can give you leads, see that you get invited to the sales conferences and site visits, and maybe even write a ticket for you now and again.

Look at it this way: When you close a $25,000 ticket with the territory wholesaler's help, he makes his override. When you close a $25,000 ticket without the wholesaler's help, *he still makes his override.* Now would you ever mount a major RELP prospecting effort without one of these people chained to your desk? We hope not.

Incidentally, sometimes you may find yourself in a situation where you think you're genuinely doing everything in your power to learn to sell a RELP proficiently. But the wholesaler whose help you've enlisted isn't holding up his end. By all means *turn him in.* Go to your office manager, or to your firm's internal RELP wholesaler, and say: "Look, if you think I'm making unreasonable demands on this person's time and energy, please tell me. I'll lay off. But it feels to me like I'm knocking myself out to produce for this guy, and all I'm doing is developing a meaningful relationship with his answering machine."

Then watch how fast you get some action. Remember, one big thing you have going for you is that the RELP business has become so crowded and competitive. Sponsors can't tolerate an ineffective wholesaler because they know another RELP's effective wholesaler will jump into the vacuum and eat their lunch. But they may not know their guy is dogging it until somebody (in this case, you) blows the whistle. So don't be shy about it (but don't go off half-cocked, either). You may be helping a lot of other producers as well as yourself.

BUILD A NETWORK

Once you're committed to building your prospecting skills by showing a particular RELP, you should think about establishing some kind of a networking arrangement with other people whose goals are similar to yours.

The RELP marketers in your firm, as well as the wholesalers who represent the RELP, can put you in touch with other salespeople in other offices of your company who've expressed an interest in working on (or who are already having success in) your particular RELP. You can also meet these people, and swap ideas with them, at area or regional sales/due diligence meetings put on by the sponsor.

You absolutely must make a point to attend these types of meetings, by the way, whenever the opportunity arises. If you really are committed to a RELP, the things you can learn are tremendous. And that lets you say to your prospects, "I met with the top executives of this RELP late last month, and they are convinced that . . . "

Networking also gives you the chance to establish prospecting games with other salespeople. For instance, suppose you want to be making two presentations of your RELP each day. Get to know someone with the same goal. You can increase your chances of success and his by contracting to pay each other $10 per uncompleted call, payable at the end of each week. See if that doesn't motivate you to make those last couple of presentations every week.

But, most importantly, networking gives you and the other participants the opportunity to have a weekly conference call. Here you trade sales ideas, objections, questions and answers, war stories and general encouragement. This reinforcement makes it so much easier to sustain a long-term prospecting program, compared to the relative isolation and frustration of going it alone. The learning curve can be greatly shortened, and that helps you produce more sales sooner . . . and may just possibly acquaint you with colleagues and friends who can leverage each other's careers for years to come.

LEVERAGE WITH SEMINARS

Let's assume, now, that you've accepted the notion that your best approach early in a prospecting program is to leverage off the wholesaler (the RELP's or your firm's). Once you establish a relationship with a wholesaler you are comfortable with, you are ready for high gear. In addition to doing your "baseline" number of presentations every day, you can start planning a seminar. And then another. And then another. Since RELPs are essentially a "confidence" sale, **nothing builds a prospect's confidence faster than seeing a whole room full of other people like them listening to, and liking, a professionally organized seminar.**

The advantages of a properly planned seminar are manifold. First, and most important, the wholesaler makes the presentation, not you. And, of almost equal importance, the wholesaler pays for it. You can watch a professional, who has practiced hundreds of times, make a superbly organized presentation. And you can see what people react to. We call it the Nod Factor: Watch closely to see which sales points the audience nods at. And after the presentation, you watch the audience lob all their questions and objections at him (not you), and listen to how he handles them. Any would-be RELP superstar must want to do this.

Yet the fact remains that seminars are only a tool, not a panacea. They're about as effective as the people who organize them. Seminars work well in the proper context, but not at all otherwise.

First of all, a seminar will only work when you and the other salespeople in your office with whom you're organizing the seminar **build and control the audience.** Sending out 4,000 letters and putting an ad in the *Des Moines Register* isn't the way to organize a RELP seminar.

Shotgun invitations simply will not work, and you wouldn't want them to, because you have no control over the audience. With your luck, you'd pull in 120 people — a good crowd. But, the second the wholesaler was finished, a 72-year-old guy would stagger to his feet, waving his cane, and shout, "Oh, yeah? Well, I'll tell you about real estate. My father had all his savings in an apartment building in Asbury Park in 1936, and the !@x¿*! bank foreclosed. We lost everything we had. Now, *what do you say to that?*"

Or, even worse, you'll have a hotel room set up for 150 people, and 18 very nice, qualified prospects will show up. They'll look at you, at the empty chairs and at the wholesaler, and think, "How could I have been so dumb?" People will do business with you for a whole lot of reasons, but pity isn't one of them.

You and your colleagues have to agree on what kind of seminar you're going to run. You have to work *backward* from a number of people you want to talk to, *and* the place you want to talk to them, *and* what you want to talk to them about. Many variations can work — fifty people in a nice local hotel meeting room, or twenty businessmen at a buffet breakfast in your office's conference room, or whatever.

The best way to build the audience is to specify a seminar topic that speaks very directly to the concerns of the people you're trying to attract. But don't forget the purpose. A seminar should be designed to do just one thing — to communicate, in the clearest, most cogent way possible, the facts about an investment. Generic content sets the stage, articulates the concept, and establishes a need. But a specific investment must be presented in the seminar.

The seminar is not the end — the seminar is the means. It's the presentation, never the close. When the seminar ends, the host should clearly tell the audience they will be called to determine what specific investment decisions the information in the seminar may have prompted. **The work of**

a seminar is not done until all the attendees are called back and asked what investment action they would like to take.

There is no end to the creative methods by which to build seminar audiences and extend RELP sales to the "natural markets" which already exist in your office's account books. For instance, the office takes a survey of every account that's bought $25,000 of municipal bonds in the last twelve months. That master list is mailed a personal, hand-written, stamped (not postage-metered) envelope. The nicely printed invitation announces a seminar on "REAL ESTATE: THE INCOME ALTERNATIVE TO DECLINING INTEREST RATES."

Four days later, each salesperson calls his invitees, and you start building an audience. Each invitee, whether he's coming or not, is offered the opportunity to recommend one acquaintance who is not currently a client of your firm (only one, because seating is, after all, limited). Then you'll have a secretary call each person who's accepted the invitation. Do that on the day of the seminar. This reconfirming call helps assure the audience stays built.

Or, hold a seminar for all the pension, profit-sharing, IRA, Keogh and 401(k) plans in the office. Offer this topic: "REAL ESTATE: THE CORNERSTONE PENSION INVESTMENT."

For the next couple of years, as the phase-in rules regarding "passive" tax deductions kick in, you'll be able to do a seminar for all the wealthiest clients of your office on: "YOUR OLD TAX SHELTERS: WHAT THEY'RE DOING FOR YOU NOW." Particularly if your firm is involved in the manufacture of new transactions which produce taxable income you can offset against old passive losses, this ought to be a great drawing card. Every attendee should be encouraged to bring his CPA.

Speaking of CPAs, one of the things we're missing as an industry is the opportunity to do seminars which we prequalify with the state CPA societies for Continuing Professional Education (CPE) credit. As the state societies continue to stiffen their requirements for CPE work by accountants (and as the professional organizers of CPE seminars stiffen their prices), CPAs are increasingly receptive to intelligently planned seminars offered by the financial planning community.

This takes some significant extra planning, and you've got to get help from a CPA who can put you in touch with the CPE department of your state's society, but the payoff in relationship-building can be very great. This is the only exception to the rule about educational seminars, for obvious reasons. What to do the seminar on? How about: "THE IMPACT OF THE NEW TAX PROPOSALS (OR TAX LAW) ON YOUR CLIENTS' INVESTMENTS?" At the rate things are going, that ought to be a timely topic for the balance of the century.

Perhaps you'll want to establish, in the office, a program of doing real estate seminars regularly — say, four times a year. The object is to build a regular audience that looks forward to these events and steadily increases. Attendees should be encouraged to bring friends, colleagues, and other potentially interested parties.

The "progress report" meeting is easily the most productive of all seminars. The ability to hold one develops as the office has more and more clients in programs (public or private) organized by a particular RELP sponsor. Perhaps the strongest approach (and one you can get away with when you've done a lot of someone's product) is to have a sit-down dinner, with the president of the RELP sponsor as the featured speaker. All your client investors with this sponsor are invited to be guests at the dinner *provided they each bring a friend who hasn't previously invested.*

One additional word of caution about seminars: **Never, never show more than one RELP at any seminar.** You will lose the ability to stand on the conceptual fit of one RELP to a set of investor needs, and just end up inviting long, wrangling, counterproductive comparisons of fee structures, sharing arrangements, etc.

You certainly can do seminars that show a RELP as part of an investment approach. For instance, if you're doing a pension investing seminar, you might want to show zero-coupon bonds, a good corporate-bond investment trust, and a RELP. But that's about as exotic as you want to get.

Here's another point on seminars: You need a registration desk at the door, so that you're sure you have a name, address and phone number for everyone who attended. By process of elimination, the list also tells you who accepted the invitation but didn't show up. Now, you have the opportunity to call the no-shows and say, "I'm sorry you weren't able to come to our seminar last night; I really missed seeing you. The speaker gave us some insight into a rather unique way of investing in real estate. I'd like to share it with you. Could you stop in for coffee tomorrow morning?"

If you find yourself scratching your head about the whole issue of seminars (if, in other words, you and your colleagues just have no idea what kind of seminar would work best), *ask your clients.* I have a little note printed up like the one shown on page 70.

If you get enough response, of course, you can schedule seminars for virtually all the times that a cluster of people checked. Or you can fall back on the notion that the ideal speaker for the occasion couldn't come in on a Wednesday night . . . would Thursday be OK?

The "participatory democracy" approach to seminar planning has another benefit. The person who specified a Tuesday breakfast feels a certain moral responsibility to show up if, in fact, you can swing a meeting at that hour.

The last point about seminars may be the most important. "Special products," as we are pleased to call them ("tax shelters" having become passé), are a relationship-oriented sale, not a transaction-oriented sale like the purchase of 100 shares of stock. The relationship-oriented sale is a face-to-face event. Therefore, promoting a regular, easy, comfortable coming-together of salespeople and clients (as seminars do peerlessly) is to be preferred over *any* other kind of client contact.

SEMINAR SCHEDULING NOTE

Dear _____ :

   With major tax changes there will certainly be some important shifts in the way investment-grade real estate is developed, bought and sold in this country. Change always brings new opportunities. We here in the Wichita Falls office of Millbrook Securities are committed to identifying opportunities as they occur throughout the year.
   We plan to offer a series of one-hour group meetings with our clients, in order to keep you up-to-date. And we'd particularly appreciate your personal participation in one or more of these meetings.
   Will you please tell us which one of the meeting formats listed below would best suit your schedule. Thanks for your consideration.

                              Sincerely,

                              _____

____ Breakfast   8:00 a.m. - 9:00 a.m.
____ Luncheon   12:00 p.m. - 1:00 p.m.
____ Late Afternoon 5:15 p.m. - 6:15 p.m.
____ Evening   7:45 p.m. - 8:45 p.m.
Preferred Day of Week   _____

SUMMARY

- Wholesalers are your first source of "leverage" — don't be shy enlisting their aid.

- Wholesalers are paid an override for your sales whether they help you or not.

- "Networking" improves your chance of success and reinforces behavior.

- Seminars are the ultimate "leverage."

- Build the audience from the topic backwards.

- Never present more than one RELP at a seminar, although you may present, carefully, more than one product.

- The purpose of a seminar is to sell product. The seminar is the presentation, not the close.

6

Prospecting III: Verbal Skills

It's certainly not too soon, as you begin to make more and better RELP prospecting calls, to start thinking about the issue of *tone* in the prospecting and sales process. We are, after all, beginning to recommend fairly specific phrases to use, and we'll develop them further in later chapters on Presentations and Questions & Answers.

The essential thesis of this book, already repeated in a number of ways, is that RELP sales success begins with being who you are and selling what you love. So, this is the last place you'd ever find anything suggesting that, to be successful, you have to learn to speak or write like someone else.

Yet it is true, in building a highly relationship-oriented sales practice, that the question of tone — of *how* you say the things you want to say — takes on a great deal of importance. During the prospecting phase of a relationship the potential client either doesn't know you well, or isn't used to hearing you talk about RELPs. He's listening most closely to the way you are saying what you say.

Also at this time, your own nervousness is likely to show in a number of spoken ways because you don't yet know if you're going to be successful in winning the account, or in obtaining the RELP order. Your tone is critical because:

NO ONE EVER ACHIEVED RELP SUPERSTARDOM WITHOUT RECOGNIZING, AND USING, THE FACT THAT THE WAY YOU SAY WHAT YOU SAY IS MORE IMPORTANT THAN WHAT YOU SAY.

Think about it. In the first ten minutes you were reading this book, you were cautioned that the potential RELP buyer never really feels that he understands a RELP in the same way that he thinks he understands a stock, a municipal bond, or a life insurance policy. That's why **people don't, as a rule, buy RELPs from people they understand; they buy RELPs from people they believe in.**

And if, in fact, the client ends up making an act of faith in the communicator/salesperson he's talking with, then the tone and feeling the salesperson transmits must be the central issue, not the pure, intellectual truth and beauty of his RELP knowledge.

The client is listening for a combination of confidence, genuine enthusiasm for a transaction, and a real sense of concern for his (the client's) needs. He knows that you can't *prove* the RELP is going to work, any more than you can prove that a stock will go up or that a bond won't go down. *The client wants to hear how you feel.*

If this is getting a little too abstract for you, let's go back a few pages to the investor who said he was coming to your seminar, and then did a no-show. Without getting too grotesque, here is something like the sound of the average, transaction-oriented salesperson when (or if) he calls that client the next day:

"Gee, I thought you said you were coming to the seminar last night. What happened? Well, anyway, our firm is coming out with this real estate deal, and I think you ought to buy some. I'm going to send you the prospectus. Take a look at it, OK?"

What is this salesperson trying to do — give his client a guilt trip? Who cares what happened? (Suppose the client says, "My dog died?")

Next, our boy uses the deathless phrase "coming out with," which should be banned altogether from the salesperson's lexicon. He thinks his client "ought to buy some." Any particular reason?.. other than that Mr. Personality is having a slow month? He's "going to send out a prospectus." Why? To guarantee that the sale never takes place? Would any sane salesperson put a 200-page prospectus in someone's hands *before* giving him a conceptual story?

This salesperson is really saying, "I wanted to get you to the meeting so the wholesaler could close you, because I sure as hell can't. But I'll keep going through the motions. Who knows? Even though you'll never be able to figure out what this deal is, you may like it."

Now, look again at the phraseology we suggested:

"I'm sorry you weren't able to come to our seminar last night; I really missed seeing you. The speaker gave us some insight into a rather unique way of investing in real estate, and I'd like to share it with you. Could you stop in for coffee tomorrow morning?"

Now, what does the client hear? First of all, he knows he stood you up. But you're not making him fabricate a story about why he wasn't there; you're being genuinely gracious about it, even going so far as to say *he was missed*. Next he hears the speaker had a great idea about buying real estate (maybe now he really is sorry he wasn't there). But, wait, you're still offering to *share it* with him . . . and you'd like to buy him a cup of coffee in the bargain.

He will probably give you the courtesy of a hearing. If he's a real prospect, he'll see you. If he won't, he's told you (though not in so many words) he's not going to buy a RELP from you. You can take this conclusion to the bank. Don't bang your head against the wall. You have to let prospects disqualify themselves, if that's what they are determined to do.

Was there much substantive difference between the two call-backs? *There wasn't any.* Was there a difference between what the two salespeople wanted to accomplish? *There wasn't any.*

Then why is the effect of the two approaches so radically different? *Tone.* (Well, 90% tone, anyway. The other 10% was tactical: sending out the bloody prospectus versus inviting the prospect in to hear the story.)

Thinking about tone will also help you guard against one of the most distasteful and destructive habits a nervous new RELP salesperson can fall into: the use of jargon. The dangers of jargon are both stylistic and substantive. Using jargon offers you a number of different ways to destroy the relationship with a potentially good RELP client even before you reach first base.

Everybody hates it when a professional from another discipline lays jargon on them that they can't understand. (This instant generation of hostility is the opposite of what the sales process is all about.)

Picture lying there in the hospital. The doctor is saying that an arrhythmic condition in your left ventricle is being aggravated by a streptococcus infection. The resulting fluid buildup in your lungs is placing an additional strain on your aorta . . . You're thinking, "Shut up, stupid, and TELL ME IF I'M GOING TO LIVE!" To which Dr. Hippocrates muses, "Well, we'll just have to wait and see."

When you're standing in the service station on a summer Friday, and the mechanic is trying to explain the relationship between your starter, the battery, your carburetor and the transmission, all you want to know is: "WHEN CAN I DRIVE MY CAR TO THE BEACH!"

Same thing with RELPs. Your prospective client is only too aware of how little he understands about real estate, and the very last thing he wants to hear out of you is anything that sounds even remotely like:

gross rent multiplier,
cap rate,
accruing second with a 5-year bullet,
absorption rate,
triple net with CPI escalators,
Reg D,

and any other half-baked technical term you can think of.

Using jargon is only going to make the prospect mad, because that's the way the person on the receiving end of jargon *always* reacts — the same way a doctor, lawyer, mechanic or engineer makes you mad when he doesn't care enough about you to speak to you in terms you can understand.

If you're lucky, the prospect is merely annoyed. If your luck doesn't hold, he won't just sit there stewing. He'll start asking you what all the terms mean, and that's where the substantive damage is done:

SALESPERSON: *Now, the great thing about this mortgage partnership is that the investments in the fund are participating wraparound mortgage loans . . .*

PROSPECT: *What's a participating wraparound mortgage loan?*

SALESPERSON: (Eight minutes of halting, rambling "white noise," clearly showing you could no more explain a wrap loan than speak Swahili.)

PROSPECT: *Who pays the first mortgage . . . The part-*
              nership? Who's the borrower? Why doesn't
              he repay the loan? Who owes the partner-
              ship or does the partnership owe? I'm con-
              fused . . . is this like a second mortgage?

SALESPERSON: (Makes low, moaning noises as the concep-
              tual logic of the investment vanishes into
              the air like dewdrops in the sunlight of an
              August morning . . .)

Contrast the above with:

SUPERSTAR: *In this program, you make mortgage loans on*
              seasoned, successful properties. You are paid a
              competitive current interest rate. And you own
              a piece of any increase in the property's value
              from here on out. So you have the best of both
              worlds — the security and current income of a
              mortgage lender, and some of the upside poten-
              tial of a property owner.

PROSPECT: *Gee, that sounds terrific!*

We'll have a great deal more to say about tone in subsequent chapters. But the message is: Start thinking and assess-
ing where you stand with respect to tone right away.

The single most effective way to begin instantaneously to
take your own "tone temperature" is to:

START TAPING YOUR PHONE CALLS
AND PRESENTATIONS.

Hearing a tape of yourself speaking for the first time can
be a pretty jarring experience. We can't really hear what we
sound like when we're talking. That's a physiological fact as
well as a psychological reality. (Please understand that we are

recommending audiotaping here. Going straight to video-tape, first crack out of the box, might be too traumatic. Still, videotape is ultimately a very worthwhile exercise, particularly in small groups where you can critique each other and compare styles. This approach is something to think very seriously about if you can crank up that networking group we recommended a while back.)

Taping telephone conversations (so you only pick up what you sound like) with clients and prospects is the surest, fastest way to start figuring out what adjustments you need to be making. Try to record five conversations of a sales or service nature with your clients every day for a month. The subject of the calls doesn't matter. In fact, the more different topics you cover, the more rounded and accurate the picture will be of what your clients and prospects are hearing. You can easily spot any common, recurrent rough spots in your tone and start working to smooth them out.

SUMMARY

- **The way you say what you say is more important than what you say.**

- **Using jargon is a capital crime.**

- **Taping presentations is a painful but productive way to improve tone.**

7

Prospecting IV: The Last Big Ticket

In Chapter 4, we were rather cautionary about prospecting for new clients with RELPs. But there are a couple of situations extremely well suited to very aggressive cold prospecting. The tickets are big enough to warrant the struggle, and the RELP product is a way of getting into accounts that are otherwise fairly difficult to crack. One is the private placement RELP buyer, who we examine closely in Chapter 15. The other is the market for pension and profit sharing plans.

FROM IRAS TO PENSIONS: THE QUALIFIED PLAN MARKET

A prospecting effort for pension plans is a second-stage rocket: You probably can't start prospecting this market from the bottom of the learning curve. But, once you've established a consistent pattern of first-stage prospecting, you may want to look at the qualified plan market as your RELP-superstar Officer Candidate School, particularly if you've started out in the IRA market and learned something about how retirement plans work.

Pension plans are probably the last great relatively untapped RELP business source. That's because American pension plans tend to be very underfunded in real estate. The reasons are interesting, and they all add up to a very promising sales environment. First of all, Americans have historically had a great deal more faith in their currency than Europeans have. The primary reality of pension investing is that you're trying to preserve the purchasing power of people's retirement income (rather than some amount of money). Pension trustees will gravitate toward assets like real estate to the extent that they don't trust the currency. That's why you'll find 30%-40% of European pension plan assets in real estate, as opposed to only about 5%-10% in the U.S.

The growing awareness on the part of pension trustees that over time real estate consistently outperforms stocks and bonds (and isn't as volatile) has made real estate an increasingly desirable pension investment. Real estate is a very sensible way to preserve current income *and* hedge asset values against inflation, or against a big uptick in interest rates.

Pension trustees are also beginning to realize that ERISA wasn't kidding. The Employee Retirement Income Security Act of 1974 made at least two fundamental changes in the way we think about investing pension assets in this country, and the courts are showing a sure and steady willingness to back ERISA's fundamentals.

One major change was the imposition, as a matter of federal law, of the "prudent man" rule. A pension trustee is now personally liable for losses in the pension portfolio which result from not investing the funds in a manner consistent with the way a "prudent man" would manage his own money. That means no more high-flying stock trades in the pension account. More important, conscientious trustees feel they are obligated to listen to more investment alternatives than ever before.

For the potential RELP superstar, the other ERISA mandate is far more interesting: diversification. The law says you have to invest in a number of different types of investments in order to be diversified adequately against a variety of economic scenarios. And the RELP superstar interprets this to mean that you need *some* (10%? 20%?) of your pension assets in real estate.

Sponsors of RELPs have products geared toward the pension market (most notably all-cash transactions and participating mortgage partnerships). They are fully prepared to make calls and presentations to pension investment committees with you, and to help you put on seminars.

But before you arrive at this relatively advanced stage, you can start with the list of people you successfully prospected on their IRA. Once someone has made a RELP investment in his own IRA, going back to him is easy. Ask him, "Why wouldn't real estate make sense for the pension plan of the company where you work? Would you be kind enough to put me in touch with the person there who looks at pension investments?" You only have to turn that trick once to write a bigger ticket than all the IRA sales you made in your first sales campaign put together. And what an account you'll have opened!

Next, you can speak to everyone in your account book whose IRA you don't have yet. Ask each person if he is a trustee of the pension plan where he works, or if he'll give you the name of someone who is. When you call you can say, "I was speaking to my client Byron Brown the other day about some work I've been doing in advising pension plans on real estate opportunities. Byron suggested that I give you a call." Then ask:

"Do you have income-producing real estate in your pension portfolio yet?"

This question is phrased so that the answer doesn't matter: If the trustee says no, do a one-minute conceptual rundown on the benefits of real estate (do *not* mention a product), and say that you make a particular specialty of matching pension plans to appropriate real estate investments. Then ask for twenty minutes — and assure him it will be no more — over coffee one morning to explore where the fit might be.

If the trustee says send him something, tell him you have nothing on the calendar at the moment, which is why you have time to make some introductory calls like this. Then ask for the coffee date again. If he demurs, say thanks and excuse yourself. Chuck the name, or file it and call him back six weeks later on zeros. No appointment, no RELP prospect.

If, on the other hand, the trustee says, "Yes, I have real estate in the account," compliment the decision. To open the discussion, ask him politely what they bought and see if you can make the coffee date to talk about a couple of interesting new concepts in pension-plan real estate investing. Same tactics: no appointment, no RELP prospect.

When you've finished this initial pension plan prospecting program, you will start to feel more comfortable in the pension market. Then, you can plan a set number of cold calls each day to companies listed in the Yellow Pages. When you call, ask the switchboard operator if you can speak to the person in charge of the company's pension or profit sharing plan.

If the operator is no help, ask just to speak to the company's treasurer. **At no time during your conversation with the operator is it necessary for you to identify yourself.** You'll be asked that soon enough.

When you're put through to someone, check that the operator understood your question by asking if this person is in charge of looking at pension plan investments. (Note that the word "investments" is not used with the operator but is introduced when you get through to the next level.) If he's not, ask for the name of the person who is. When you're sure you're talking to the right person, simply ask your "Do you have income-producing real estate . . . " question again. Then follow the same format outlined above, and go for the coffee date. Again: no appointment, no prospect.

If you're going to work successfully in the pension market without cracking up, one thing you have to remember is that the pension investment decision can be a very long, and perhaps committee-dominated, process. It's just not the kind of situation where you go in, meet one-on-one with the decision-maker, make a great presentation, answer some questions, and walk out with signed paperwork and a check.

The pension business is also phenomenally wholesaler intensive. The trustees just feel better if the third-party expert, who is an officer of the RELP sponsor, comes in to answer technical questions, hold their hands, and generally help them thicken their due diligence file (remember the "prudent man" rule). You have to adjust your pace and your style to this approach. If you can, you'll be well rewarded. The size of the tickets you'll write will amply repay you for your patience, not to speak of the amount of product knowledge and sales skill you'll pick up from watching a professional operate.

The pension business can create relationships for you with not one, but several top people in a company — relationships you can begin to capitalize on, in time, by turning to the question of their personal investing.

No matter how you approach the pension market, though, only one approach really matters: You have to make a commitment to some sustainable, long-term, daily call schedule. That's the only way you are going to succeed.

SUMMARY

- Real estate is a suitable investment for qualified pension plans, and pension funds probably ought to buy more real estate.

- The sales process is lengthy and wholesaler-intensive. BE PATIENT.

- The benefits are big tickets and rapid progress on the learning curve.

- Like all other prospecting, it is a numbers game.

8

Presentations I:
Theory and Presentation Points

Dr. Edward Teller, the father of the hydrogen bomb and one of the most distinguished scientists of this century, gave a series of lectures at Pepperdine University in the spring of 1978; he spoke about modern science, with a particular eye toward the human consequences of scientific endeavor. In time, the lectures were collected into a book. Dr. Teller entitled the book *The Pursuit of Simplicity*.

Miles Davis is the greatest jazz musician of the postwar era and a man who has changed the shape of jazz not once, but two or three times in the last thirty years. Davis gave a rare interview that was published in the *New York Times Magazine* in 1985. Here's what he said goes through his mind when he listens to his own music: "I always listen to what I can leave out."

In August of 1978, just after Pete Rose ended his forty-four game hitting streak, Thomas Boswell of *The Washington Post* (maybe America's premier baseball writer) wrote of Rose: "Extraordinary men often bring a fresh simplicity to the complexity of their chosen fields."

And, in a 1985 feature in *Art and Antiques* magazine, the painter Andrew Wyeth ("Christina's World") said of his art: "The less subject matter in a picture, the better. If you can express it by just one thing, it's that much better."

Perhaps the most interesting comment on the notion that less is more was written nearly two hundred years ago by Thomas Jefferson, himself one of the greatest prose stylists in our language. In talking about two of his contemporaries, he made an astounding observation:

> *"I served with General Washington in the legislature of Virginia before the Revolution, and during it with Dr. Franklin in Congress. I never heard either of them speak ten minutes at a time, nor to any but the main point that was to decide the question. They laid their shoulders to the great points, knowing that the little ones would follow of themselves."*

What does all of this have to do with RELP sales presentations? Only everything, that's all. You are hearing from and about this diverse group of supremely accomplished people that the quality distinguishing their work — the one thing that makes them ingenious where others are merely competent — is a classic:

SIMPLICITY.

The essence of all the great sales presentations you have heard in your whole career is . . . simplicity. **In every great sales presentation you've ever heard, the logic was laid out in a way that seemed effortless.**

Well, the presentation wasn't effortless to put together. And between now and the point where you emerge as a RELP superstar — in other words, when *your* presentations make people smile and say, "Hey, that's great, and you made it so easy for me to understand" — you have an awful lot of work to do.

But we hope you've caught on by now that the work isn't the kind you were afraid you were facing: endless study of tax law, real estate finance, deal structure, accounting and all those other *facts*. Once again, knowledge of those facts will surely come in time, as you continue to practice the craft of being a RELP communicator/salesperson. The work you have cut out for you is far more important, because you're slowly beginning to accept the great truth that:

NO ONE EVER BECAME
A GREAT SALESPERSON OF ANYTHING
UNTIL HE LEARNED
TO TRANSCEND THE FACTS.

The great cellist Pablo Casals gave a "master class" near his home in Puerto Rico during the last years of his life. A master class is for people who have studied an instrument all their lives at the finest music schools with the best teachers, and who are now almost ready to take their places in the very first rank of musicians in the world. Their training is completed with one of the greatest living masters.

The first thing Casals said on the first morning of class was, "Now, we must please forget the notes." He was saying, of course, "You know the music; you have all the technical proficiency you need or you wouldn't be here. Now, if you're to become *artists*, you have to get beyond all that stuff."

Well, you haven't got all the technical proficiency yet, but the principle is the same.

In Chapter 2, we suggested that RELPS are at least as simple as other investments in which you deal, comfortably and effectively, every day. In fact, we went so far as to say then — and we repeat now — **a RELP with more than three absolutely critical issues is the exception, not the rule.** The difficulty, we suggested, is that in explaining a RELP, you tend to suspend the awesome powers of assumption and simplification you use so effortlessly in selling other investments. With RELPs you try to carry the day with a mass of facts and figures you heard in a sales meeting, 70% of which are probably *extraneous* to the investment decision-making process.

THE FIVE-POINT PRESENTATION RULE

What you need is a method with which to build up your powers of simplification in RELPs. This is kind of a RELP-superstar-in-training Nautilus workout in reverse: As you get better, instead of doing or saying *more,* you do and say *less.* And here it is:

**FROM THIS MOMENT ON,
WHEN YOU'RE PRESENTING A RELP,
YOU'RE NOT ALLOWED TO TELL YOUR PROSPECT
MORE THAN FIVE POINTS
(THREE, IF THE PRESENTATION IS BY PHONE).**

That's for the first year of RELP sales, when (as you remember) you are going to make at least one presentation every day, even if it's only to an IRA. At the beginning of the second year, your limit drops down to four points in person/three on the phone. And, in year three, when it all comes together (and you can be absolutely sure, if you follow the path in this book, that it will), you are only going to communicate three main points in person or on the phone.

The reasoning behind the five-point limitation is essentially the one word we hope you remembered from the first part of this chapter, SIMPLICITY. In an initial presentation, five points of first-rank importance are all a client *needs* to know. Granted, he may *want* to know more, and when he does, he'll ask you. But, be assured the sun has never shone on the RELP having more than five supremely important issues.

Five points face-to-face, and three on the phone, are the absolute limit of what the normal mind can process in one feeding. Remember, the person you're talking to feels keenly his lack of any in-depth real estate knowledge. So an extra effort is required for him to get his arms around even the few points you want to tell him. Beyond that, his circuits are overloaded, and you lose him. (In fact, one school of thought says that you can't tell anyone more than three things about *anything!*)

The five-point limitation is every bit as important to the emerging RELP superstar as it is to his prospect. Because what we're trying to do here is encourage the salesperson to overcome his own anxieties and to build his own confidence.

Most of us salespeople are pretty verbal to begin with. Verbal people tend to talk too much when they're nervous. In dealing with RELPs, you don't feel as easy and comfortable as you do with the other investments you sell. That discomfort tends to make you nervous. Add it all up, and chances are, when you start presenting RELPS, you're going to get nervous and end up talking too much.

Here's another thing: We all have a tendency of overcompensating when we talk about things we don't fully understand, by pouring on a lot of facts we do know. The result is the same: We talk too much, and the client is hopelessly confused.

Finally, we all have a subconscious dread that when (and if) we ever stop talking, the client is going to ask a question we can't answer. (You can stop worrying about that one, because, as promised earlier, *he will.*)

The Five-Point Presentation Rule is to encourage you, instead, to make short, intensely logical and very carefully practiced presentations of the few really key elements in your RELP. In tennis, you cannot lose a point *when the ball is in your opponent's court.* In RELP selling, you can't foul up your presentation, or confuse your client and yourself, *when you have stopped talking.*

Besides, the major conceptual issues in any transaction are the clearest and easiest to communicate. You may just express the overwhelming logic of those points so satisfyingly that the client's nagging concern about nitpicky secondary and tertiary questions evaporates. The client might even say, "Oh, I get it. Sure, that makes good sense." But you will never know until you shut up.

YOU CANNOT LEARN ANYTHING ABOUT WHAT'S WORRYING YOUR CLIENT UNTIL YOU STOP TALKING.

So the object of this chapter is to get you to sit down with your clients and, in the quietest, most direct and least complicated way possible, make the best presentation you've ever made. All this exercise can do, though, is to prepare you for the presentation itself . . . nothing can prepare you for the surprise and delight with which prospects respond to simple clarity.

Look at it from the prospect's viewpoint. If your prospect is daunted, and a little on his guard, because he realizes he doesn't understand real estate, he'll be intensely grateful to you for purifying the critical factors down to a precious, comprehensible few.

The busiest, most successful people (who can, and often want to, make serious RELP investments) have pressing demands on their time and attention. They couldn't, even if they wanted to, slow up long enough to analyze your RELP recommendation in minute detail. Their reaction is extremely positive if you put them in a position to make a perfectly intelligent judgment very quickly. You show you are a professional who cares enough about them to reduce the investment to its essential elements.

Then, if it turns out that your RELP isn't the right answer for them, they'll tell you quickly and appreciatively why they don't think the RELP fits. Far from rejecting you, they will actually be telling you what, if anything, they would really like to own.

How do you pick your five world-class presentation points? Call your internal RELP marketing person, as well as the RELP's wholesaler, and ask:

"What five points would you have me tell my clients, to the exclusion of all others, in order to induce them correctly to make this investment?"

When they recover from the shock of being asked so intelligent and pointed a question, they'll probably have some extremely interesting things to say. They may even, in a burst of creativity, work up more than five essential elements in the superiority of the RELP. Don't permit it.

Discipline them, as you're prepared to discipline yourself. Have them think through the question of what is the basic, irreducible logic of the investment.

Now, with their Favorite Five, you can work up a clear, logical, compelling arrangement of the points . . . and then *start practicing*. Tape your presentation again and again. Role-play with the wholesalers; role-play with your networking group (incidentally, what are their five points?). Grind it, polish it, and just make it as tight and seamless as you can. Because:

THE ACT OF PERFECTING A SALES PRESENTATION IS MORE BENEFICIAL THAN ALL THE PRODUCT-KNOWLEDGE SESSIONS IN THE WORLD.

Well, sure it is. You know that the fifth or tenth time you hear a story, you are able to chip away at it, to pick holes in it, to formulate questions the presentation just doesn't answer.

Practicing so that you can spot those flaws and inconsistencies may prompt you to tighten the presentation even further. Or, as you begin to approach RELP superstardom, you may even consciously decide to leave some rough spots in the presentation because you'll know exactly what questions they provoke. And, you'll know just how terrific your answers are!

Your objective is to get so good you can be shaken out of a sound sleep and be making the presentation, with the utmost warmth and conviction, before your feet hit the floor.

When you get that good, you can actually begin to detach yourself from the presentation, to let the force of painstakingly acquired habit take over, and to **devote your real attention to watching the prospect's reactions.** Remember the Nod Factor? We said that, during a seminar, you can observe which points in the wholesaler's presentation the audience is reacting to. Well, the next step in your presentation progress is actually to be able to observe the client's reactions to what you're saying. (A pro can adjust for, and anticipate, those reactions, even while speaking.)

The seamless beauty of your presentation can, after all, only take you so far. In the end, what you said doesn't matter, only how the client reacted to what you said. (There's a glimpse of the issue of tone again.) Having a perfectly rehearsed presentation enables you to tune yourself out, and start watching the prospect's reactions.

SUGGESTIONS FOR YOUR FIVE KEY POINTS

What are the five points you're going to make in your superstar presentation? The answer has to be tailor-made to fit the RELP and your style. The specific points will be decided by you and your colleagues — the internal wholesaler and the RELP wholesaler. You've got to let the points flow, not from some rigid formula in a book, but from your sense of the real, natural superiority of the RELP you fall in love with.

Having said that, however, we have some strong suggestions of things which you may want to build your presentation around.

(1) **THE CONCEPT** — THE CONCEPT is an opening statement defining the *need* which you perceive in your client's situation. It contains a statement, in generic terms, of how a particular type of real estate investment has historically met that need.

Without a doubt, articulating THE CONCEPT is the one critical, indispensable way to begin any financial services presentation, if only because the client's reaction will instantly tell you if you're on the right track. Very few people, when presented with a statement of what they genuinely need to accomplish will (or would even want to) mask the depth of feeling with which they agree with you. On the other hand, a prospect will probably stop you right away if you're wrong, which will save you a lot of time and energy.

Say you start with, "You're 42 years old, making $120,000 a year and adequately insured. What you need is to build real assets by seeking maximum appreciation." The prospect may say, "No, no, I'm running my 79-year-old mother's trust fund, and the bond portfolio isn't producing enough income." You just spared yourself an agonizing twenty minutes and an awful lot of embarrassment.

When the prospect nods vigorously at your statement of need, you already have him agreeing with you. And you haven't said a word about product yet, nor should you. Instead, you'll want to say something to the effect that leveraged equity real estate ownership is one proven way of building assets while creating a tax-free income stream. Not "the only" way, nor even "the best" way, but "one proven way." Once again, you're selling exposure, not proof.

In the next chapter, we'll suggest a precisely-worded concept presentation for each major type of public real estate partnership, and later we'll offer one for private placements.

For now, just remember that Point One of your five-point RELP presentation should be THE CONCEPT: a short summary of your understanding of a major financial goal of your prospect, together with the matching goals of a particular form of real estate investing.

(2) **THE GENERAL PARTNER** — Another item we recommend as a key presentation point is a strong statement about the general partner and, particularly if it's appropriate, about your firm's relationship with the general partner. In the end, the identity, character, business acumen and financial strength of a RELP's general partner are the critical issues that determine the success of your investment.

Real estate, after all, performs about as well as it is managed. You buy real estate on one day, and you sell it another day. But you manage real estate every day in between. The best built, best located, best financed real estate investment anywhere can have problems or underperform with the wrong management.

One of the best things you can stress is the extent to which you personally have been exposed to the general partner's management, and to property they have previously bought. If the general partner owns or has built property in an area your prospect would know, by all means mention it. Any special aspect of the real estate business at which the general partner is particularly skilled is also fair game.

Always watch your time and *never* lapse into jargon. Remember that you are simply feeding the prospect some general confidence-building ideas. You are letting the prospect sense your commitment to, and depth of feeling for, the general partner. And you are giving him a sense of your enthusiasm for the general partner's uniqueness.

Don't hide behind words like "biggest" and "best," either. The prospect usually starts to feel that he's being hyped, and you really aren't giving him any feeling for why you like this particular general partner. The investor knows that "big" can work against him as well as for him; he also knows that large or small operators can concentrate on doing one thing, or working one territory, supremely well. "Best" is immeasurable, a subjective value judgment. The issue is tone, again. Do you want to sound like someone who brings good people together, or do you want to sound like a car salesman?

Incidentally, making a big thing out of the general partner's track record, oddly enough, is a fairly dangerous tack. In the first place, it's the wrong way to appeal to a prospect. You should be inducing your prospect to invest his confidence in you, and, through you, in the general partner. Talk about the management personnel of the general partner whom you know. Talk about your firm's relationship with them. Talk about how comfortable your other clients are who own other deals from the same general partner. Don't hide behind a table of essentially incomprehensible, cold numbers you probably don't understand anyway.

Beyond that, the real danger lies in all the suspicions and questions talking about a track record seems to unleash. Just count the number of absolute show-stoppers that you may provoke if you say, "And here you can clearly see that the nine properties they have previously sold produced an after-tax internal rate of return of 28.6%":

(1) *What's an internal rate of return?*
(2) *Sure, they sell the ones that go up; they probably keep the dogs so you can't see them.*
(3) *Well, that was California in the '70s. Inflation was wild and everything quintupled. There's no inflation now, and besides, they're buying office buildings in Bloomfield Hills, Michigan. Apples and oranges.*
(4) *A lot of that was tax benefits that the "new tax law" is taking away. What did the investors make in cash?*
(5) *What does the footnote mean about taking back notes from the buyer of the property? You mean the investor is not really out? Suppose the new guy doesn't pay?*

(6) If they can make this much money, what do they need me for?

(7) Let's see, that's about four times the return I'm getting on municipal bonds now. So, I guess real estate is about 400% riskier than muni's, right?

Don't do it! The track record is there if you ever need it, but only discuss specifics when responding to a direct question.

PROSPECT: Jim, you say your RELP has produced consistently superior returns. Is that documented anywhere?

SUPERSTAR: Yes, Mr. Prospect, to some extent it is. We have the complete history on nine properties which have gone through the entire investment cycle and have been sold. These properties represented, at the time they were sold, $10 million of total value. Total return to the investor averaged around 28% a year, including the tax benefits. There's no guarantee they can go on producing such excellent results, I guess, but it is a significant record of accomplishment."

All selling that hides behind numbers is essentially weak. Selling track record is particularly weak. Winners sell opportunity and relationships; losers sell (or, more accurately, try and fail to sell) "proof." And, if the prospect doesn't ask detailed questions about track record, you never have to tapdance into that quagmire at all.

(3) & (4) **THE RELP ITSELF AND ITS INVESTMENT OBJECTIVES** — The RELP is the investment solution you've chosen for the needs outlined in THE CONCEPT. Remember, you never begin with the RELP. You need to follow a road map to the RELP. Start by identifying a particular financial planning concern the prospect has. Show generically

how good quality real estate may help solve the problem. Introduce the general partner with whom you and your firm have a particularly comfortable relationship, and whose style of real estate investing is consistent with your prospect's goals. Then, finally, present the deal.

Starting with the RELP, no matter how much you may love it, is like trying to climb a glacier in tennis shoes. Instead, build logically into the deal by way of THE CONCEPT and the people. Then the deal becomes what it deserves to be — the means to the end, rather than the end in itself.

Waiting to introduce the deal also drains a lot of "burden of proof" out of the situation when you arrive at the point of presenting your RELP, because you've built a pattern of general agreement with the prospect by asking him, at each major point, whether he's still comfortably with you. And he's been saying things like, "Yes, that's a good description of my need." "Yes, I can see how real estate ownership, in the way you're describing it, might help solve my problem." "Yes, those seem like experienced and level-headed people."

When you arrive at the point of describing the RELP, make the presentation as economically, honestly and fairly as you can. There's no point regurgitating the dozen points you heard in a long sales meeting. Simply state the kinds of properties the partnership is buying/lending on; when cash flow should start and at what level (always an estimate, never a "pegged" number); what level of tax protection, if any, the program may produce; and try to give your prospect some feeling for your RELP's anticipated holding period (particularly if you think you're selling against bonds and CDs).

Make absolutely no estimates as to upside potential. You can't, because you don't know. Your prospect knows you don't know. That's Ok, because no one else knows either. Stand on the issues of investment diversification and a well-documented history of real estate outperforming other investments.

The great advantage of making the presentation in this manner is that it presumes acceptance by the prospect. In a simple, understated way it says: "We agree on what your need is, and we agree that real estate can help. This vehicle is the obvious choice. I won't bore you with the details."

That's the opposite of what most people's presentations do, strange as it may seem. Without realizing it, RELP salespeople think, "I love this RELP, and I know it's right for this prospect." But then they concentrate on stating all the right facts to convince the prospect of how good the RELP is . . . without laying the conceptual foundation first.

The RELP superstar says, "I understand this prospect so well, I can define any need he has. Real estate can fill any need. The RELP I select is so perfect for my prospect, that he's *inevitably* going to see the wisdom of making the investment with me."

What's the essential difference between the two approaches? To an amazing degree, it's in how many things you try to tell your prospect:

**THE MORE YOU THINK YOU HAVE
TO TELL YOUR PROSPECT,
THE LESS CONFIDENT YOU APPEAR,
AND THE MORE THE PROSPECT WONDERS WHY
YOU FEEL YOU HAVE TO SELL SO HARD.**

The trademarks of the RELP superstar are economy of dialogue, simplicity in presentation, and the presumption of the ability to generate understanding and to succeed. Don't worry. If you leave something out, or fail to cover something your prospect wants to know about, he'll ask you.

Two more strong recommendations complete our general advice about presenting the RELP. **Never state the attributes of the RELP in terms of what it is not.** Statements like the following are counterproductive: "This RELP does not take back paper." "This private placement isn't marked up with a wrap mortgage payable to the GP." "This isn't one of those triple-net leased shopping centers with no upside potential." You are using jargon and reminding the prospect about his greatest fear, his lack of real understanding of RELPs. If the client is worried about something in the transaction, he'll ask. Express yourself in terms of positives, not in terms of things that can only frighten your prospect.

Second, never state the sharing arrangements (the split of tax and economic benefits between the general partner and the limited partner investor). Sharing arrangements make most investors' eyes glaze over. Again, if the client cares to know, he'll ask. Then be prepared to tell him a lot of nifty things about the superiority of your general partner's style of sharing costs and revenues. The greatest sharing arrangement in the world will not make bad real estate good, or make a dumb property manager smart. Investors care most about the management and the properties. Remember that in your initial presentation you have to stay with the big picture. The sharing arrangement is a secondary issue.

(5) **THE RISK** — Always make some reference to risk in your five-point presentation. Doing so is extremely disarming, as well as genuinely comforting. The prospect can see clearly that you are not just another salesperson painting an unreasonably rosy picture. The communicator/salesperson who makes some cogent reference to risk *without being asked* usually scores on two separate counts: The prospect sees that yours is a realistic and professional approach, because he knows that any investment has risk. Second, you get to point out how the general partner takes steps to manage the risk, which has the effect of looping the discussion back into the strength of the GP.

No reasonable investor thinks any investment is without risk. He wants to know how risks are recognized and dealt with effectively. The RELP superstar always goes on the offensive in raising the issue of risk. He can only gain his prospects' respect, and he never exposes himself to being in a defensive posture when asked, as he inevitably will be, "What are the risks?"

The message of this chapter is that whatever RELP you choose can be presented with an effective, generic, universally adaptable approach. Learn the basic principles. You won't run the risk of being a "one-trick pony." You'll be able to sell across the whole spectrum of RELPs because you can fit any individual RELP story into the same, easy presentation formula.

SUMMARY

- The essence of all great sales presentations is simplicity.

- No one ever became a great salesperson of anything until he learned to transcend the facts.

- Make the presentation with no more than five points, because there aren't any more critical issues than that, and because the prospect can only absorb a limited amount of information.

- A short presentation helps you control your own nervousness and helps find out what's worrying your client when you stop talking.

- Practice your presentation until you can make it without thinking. Then watch your client's reactions.

- Build your five points from:
  (a) THE CONCEPT,
  (b) the General Partner,
  (c) the RELP itself,
  (d) the RELP's investment objectives, and
  (e) the Risk, and how it's managed.

- Operate on the presumption of success. Things generally turn out the way you really believe they will.

9

Presentations II: Techniques

Economizing your presentation down to five stated points (spoken, as you'll see, over no more than about five minutes) isn't easy. When you've accomplished it, you'll be so proud of the way you can lay out the logic of any RELP that you may be genuinely surprised, and somewhat put off, if your prospect interrupts with a question.

That's upsetting, to be sure. And, if you've worked as hard as you should on refining your presentation down to its clear and most logical essence, you really don't *deserve* to be interrupted. You'll feel, with a lot of justification, that the prospect should keep still and let you set out the logic the way you want to. He won't have to wait that long for Q&A, because your presentation is so short. You are convinced he'll quickly see the logic in its completeness. Thus, he'll already be over the hump and on the downhill side of the decision-making process.

The trouble is, you can't tell him that he can't interrupt. You can't explain to him that the best course of action for him is to hold his questions so you can give him the whole story in one clip. You just can't do it.

It's only human nature, after all, to ask a question when one occurs to you. And the more successful, accomplished and intense your prospect is, the more incapable he may be of sitting back and letting you unfold your presentation at your own practiced pace. Hence, he may break in at any time with a question or observation that he's clearly requiring you to comment on.

So what you may want to do is to resort to a little diplomatic delaying tactic. When your prospect can no longer contain himself and breaks in with a question, hold up a hand, nod *very* acceptingly, and say:

"I'm coming to that."

If you *are* coming to that (if he's raising something that genuinely appears later on in your presentation), so much the better. More often than not, however, you won't be coming to that specific point in your initial presentation. So the use of the phrase "I'm coming to that" takes on a gentle air of subterfuge — subterfuge in a good cause, mind you, that will ultimately be very useful to you *and* the client. But subterfuge nonetheless, and that demands a momentary digression.

You've just read the first and last recommendation in this book that you employ anything but the most sincere, direct and honest statements and tactics. Salespeople who feel they have to slant the facts, or overweigh the positives versus the negatives, or not state the negatives at all, or manipulate their clients in any way, end up very unhappy people (if they're not already). And they leave a fair amount of human and financial damage in their wake.

The worst part of manipulative selling, though, is that *you* end up hurt. Elbert Hubbard said it best: "Men are not so much punished *for* their sins as *by* them." You carry the result of being less than honest with your clients around with you, and the cumulative effect, consciously or unconsciously, will really shrivel you up.

Do you say, "Well, I had to overstate because that's the only way I could ever get this jerk to make up his mind?"

Well, we suggest you don't like this client. What's worse, you don't believe in your own capacity to reach him honestly. Stop calling him. He's hurting you by making you dislike both him *and* yourself.

Salespeople who accumulate a book of accounts they don't like, or even respect, are really piling up a lot of psychological conflict. What's worse, they're constructing a world of associates for whom they feel hostility and disdain. But, as Emerson tells us, "People seem not to see that their opinion of the world is also a confession of character." Try to remember: You are how you feel about your clients. (Ok, Ok, end of sermon.)

You've just said, "I'm coming to that," primarily to hold your prospect still for the few more minutes you'll take to finish your presentation. And he can't (or at least in most instances, won't) argue with that. So the first benefit is that "I'm coming to that" lets you get through your presentation without having the conceptual logic chopped up.

But that's not all. If, in fact, you do not return to the question your prospect asked, then:

"I'M COMING TO THAT" WILL TELL YOU, WITH UNERRING ACCURACY, WHETHER THE PROSPECT REALLY CARES ABOUT THE QUESTION.

How? Simple. If the question is really bothering the prospect, and you don't return to it, he'll ask you the question again. Then, and only then, do you treat it as a serious issue.

Most of the time you'll never hear the question again, which says about the prospect:

(1) He figured out the answer; or
(2) He grasped the overriding conceptual logic of why you love this RELP for him, so he stopped caring about his question; or

(3) His question never mattered in the first place. He was just constitutionally incapable of sitting there, in his plush, intimidating office, letting *you* control the agenda. That's human nature. And you handled the situation in a *very* nice way.

Let's spend another minute on the issue of control. Remember, after you've settled in with your client, gotten your coffee and come to the business at hand:

THE PERIOD OF YOUR GREATEST CONTROL OVER YOUR CLIENT'S IMPRESSIONS OF YOU AND YOUR PRODUCT IS DURING YOUR PRESENTATION.

While you're making your presentation, you're beaming a steady impression of confidence, which is *the* essential element in the RELP sale. Sometime during the presentation, you must have the prospect realize, "Hey, this salesperson believes in what he's selling just as much as I believe in what I do. I may not accept what he's saying yet (I may still have a lot of questions) but this guy is no peddler, he's no lightweight, and he's sincere. Hmmm . . . "

What is the prospect listening to at that moment? You guessed it: He's listening to the *way* you're saying what you're saying more than he's listening to what you're saying. Heard that before? While you have control, you have to accomplish as much as you can.

Your presentation is your cleanest, best shot. Because, in a moment, you'll have to start giving up control as the interview moves on to Q&A. The sale can't begin until the customer starts asking questions. You have to accept that Q&A is where the rubber meets the road. Make the very best opening statement you can in order to condition the prospect's mind in as favorable a way as possible.

The stronger, surer and more concise your presentation is, the more you can be certain that you've shaken up the prospect's thinking. That way, he may see beyond the relatively unimportant issue of the RELP you're presenting to the paramount issue of the kind of professional you are (because, first and foremost, you're selling yourself).

What if, after your best and most deeply felt presentation, the prospect turns a deaf ear not just to the deal but to *you?* If you're prospecting right, this rejection will happen to you less and less. If you can actually talk your way into a prospect's office (or talk him into coming to yours) and you're not finding any common ground on which to do business, you are not qualifying your prospects enough. There are just too many reasonable people out there — people who want, and know they need, guidance from a caring professional.

You should never have to work terribly hard to get to see someone, only to have him signal you that he's never going to do business with you. **You have to let prospects disqualify themselves if that's what they've made up their minds to do.**

A slow form of suicide is the act of trying desperately to sell somebody when he clearly and steadfastly is refusing to be sold. Life is too short; your reserves of sales energy are not limitless. Spend your energy generating new, more reasonable prospects rather than desperately clutching at a few marginal ones, just because they are the prospects you have.

NO ONE EVER ACHIEVED "SPECIAL PRODUCTS" STARDOM UNTIL HE REALIZED, AND FULLY ACCEPTED, THAT HIS SERVICES WERE THE BEST THING THAT HAD HAPPENED TO HIS CLIENTS IN YEARS.

Alfred North Whitehead put it another way, and his version is chiseled into the cornerstone of the Columbia School of Business: "A great society is one whose men of business think greatly of their functions." That's it. Unless you have a firmly fixed conviction you are doing a terrific job finding sensible real estate solutions to clients' needs, you aren't going to make it. If, deep down, you feel you're just another journeyman salesperson trying for a share of the RELP sales pie like everybody else, forget it. Either sell RELPs that you really love, or . . . sell something else.

That's why it's so sad to hear salespeople ask, "What's the number of times you make a presentation to a prospect before you give up?" The answer, of course, is that you never "give up." You "go on" to a more deserving prospect. The salesperson who's looking objectively for a correct number of times to call a prospect is telling you he doesn't know how to communicate with people, or to hear what they're really saying to him.

Face facts: If you've been in sales for any length of time, you should be able to tell in ten minutes whether a prospect is accepting your style of doing business. If you can't, either you should get out of sales or you are ignoring the basic fact that sales is a numbers game. You are desperately spending time talking to someone who's inflicting pain on you rather than hanging up (or walking away) and prospecting someone else.

In plain fact, salespeople put up with, and accept, about as much rejection as they think they deserve. The salesperson who, in Whitehead's words, "thinks greatly of his functions" will instantly and painlessly turn away from rejection and forge ahead in search of someone who accepts him for the fine professional that he is. If you do otherwise, you internalize the rejection. In other words, you accept that a prospect's negative reaction to you and your sales approach is somehow correct. That's a terribly sad way to live your life. No RELP superstar behaves that way.

The superstar has unshakable faith in three things:

(1) himself,
(2) his product, and
(3) the numbers.

SUMMARY

- Use "I'm coming to that" so you can make your presentation in one piece. You need to control the interview throughout the presentation.

- "I'm coming to that" filters out unimportant questions and leaves only substantive concerns.

- Your period of greatest control over your client's impressions of you and the product is during the presentation.

- Beam constantly at your prospect, communicating what a truly great job you're trying to do for him.

- Don't spend a lot of time prospecting people you don't like, or who don't seem to like you.

- Let prospects disqualify themselves.

- Respect yourself and your function, or your clients will not.

10

How to Present Leveraged Equity RELPs

When you sit down to develop a specific RELP presentation, approach it from the perspective that this is your prospect's best shot at a nontechnical, simple, comprehensible explanation. Then you can proceed to strip away the details and technicalities and go straight to the heart of the investment. That way, you can be confident that your explanation of any RELP gives the prospect his very best chance to understand it, and to see your honest enthusiasm for it.

Now all that remains is for you to accept the fact that **all your prospect really wants is a simple explanation.** The ultimate reality is that you are simplifying to serve your clients' purposes, not your own.

Seen in this way, presentation skills become indispensable, critical communication tools, *not* a way of glossing over realities to manipulate the prospect. **Your presentation skills are the only possible bridge between the complexities of real estate and the needs of the client.**

In setting up a standardized approach to presenting different kinds of RELPs, we want to use the previously established format and build out from THE CONCEPT. In formulating THE CONCEPT, we restate the investor's goals and then speak generically about how a particular type of real estate investing accomplishes the goal before we say anything about the particular RELP.

The object is simply to have the investor say yes a minimum of two important times before he hears a specific recommendation. Incidentally, all the great salespeople know that their chances of closing the sale are in direct proportion to the number of times the client says yes during a presentation. That's not manipulation. It's just plain old common sense.

Let's start with the granddaddy of all RELPs, the one that many people call "the cornerstone of a partnership investment portfolio."

LEVERAGED EQUITY REAL ESTATE

We'll restrict the discussion to publicly registered transactions, since private placements have a chapter all their own. What you're selling in public leveraged equity partnerships is, of course, the *ownership* of real estate. What you're really doing is making a cash downpayment and borrowing the great bulk of the purchase price of the properties in the form of mortgages. You are magnifying all the potential benefits of real estate ownership (as well as some of the risks) through leverage.

Leveraged equity real estate is the entry-level investment we all make in property: our home. Don't let anyone tell you he doesn't understand home ownership. But even more important, realize that everyone's personal experience with his home will, *if you allow it to,* reinforce his decision to buy a leveraged equity RELP. You are not running any risk of insulting your client's intelligence (if that's what you're worried about) by reminding him of the single best investment he ever made. Nor will you go wrong by showing him that the principles are much the same: a little bit of equity, a lot of debt, pay off the lender, and keep all the upside.

But RELPs are a much better way to buy leveraged real estate (putting aside, of course, the fact that you need someplace to sleep). First of all, the costs of buying a RELP are less than the costs of buying a house. (We'll save the explanation for the "Q&A" chapter.) Second, you depreciate the property in your RELP, because rental property is a business; you can't depreciate your personal residence. Third, the mortgage is paid down from rental income, not from the sweat of *your* brow. And last, if your RELP can't pay the mortgage, you can walk away into the sunset scot-free. The upside potential was leveraged, yet the downside was "nonrecourse," as they say.

For the great majority of investors considering a RELP for their personal account, leveraged equity is the way to go. (Not always so for their IRA or pension accounts, but stay tuned.)

Before trying to work up a conceptual presentation for this RELP type, let's get squared away on a few mechanical details.

The more leverage you're using:

- the more tax deductions per investment dollar,
- the more upside potential you have;
- the less cash flow you get in the early years; and
- the more risk you're taking.

(If this is too simplistic for you, feel free to skip ahead. We won't be offended.) Why more tax deductions? Let's compare a RELP that's 50% leveraged to one that's 80% leveraged. In other words, in the first one you put up $.50 and borrow $.50 for each dollar paid to purchase the property; in the other, you put up $.20 and borrow $.80.

Both own $1.00 of property, so over a number of years you will write off (deduct) roughly $1.00 in depreciation. One dollar of deductions is twice the $.50 downpayment in the first example but **five times** the downstroke in the deal with only $.20 of equity. Case closed: Higher leverage, higher depreciation in relation to equity.

Now, why does higher leverage mean more upside potential? Imagine that in each case $1.00 of property appreciates at 6% a year for 5 years. Through the magic of compounding, each property is now worth $1.34. So you sell and pay off the mortgages. After paying the $.50 you owe on the low-leverage property, your $.50 equity investment has turned into $.84 ($1.34 less $.50 of debt). Your gain was 68%. Not too shabby.

But look at what happens in the high-leverage case. When you pay off the $.80 you owe there, your $.20 equity investment has turned into $.54 ($1.34 less $.80 of debt), a whopping 170% increase! Please note the two properties performed the same; the difference in percentage gain on equity was all in the leverage.

Now, what's the bad news? Well, first of all, more leverage means less cash flow. Real estate trades on its yield, right? So let's say the $1.00 property earns $.08 in cash flow, before you consider the mortgage payments. In other words, your real estate investment yields 8% before debt service. (Surprise! We just sneaked into this extremely nontechnical tome a nontechnical illustration of "cap rate!" The hypothetical property was bought on an 8% "cap rate"; that is, the net operating income before debt service yields 8% to the buyer. Please don't tell anybody you read about cap rate here, or this book might lose its amateur standing among product knowledge lovers.)

Now, let's assume the mortgage debt bears interest at 10%. The $.50 mortgage requires a nickel in interest per year (forget about principal for a minute). So $.08 in operating income less a nickel in debt service leaves us a net cash flow of $.03 a year. In the other case, the $.80 mortgage requires $.08 in interest; all the operating income pays annual interest, leaving no cash flow at all. there you are: the higher the leverage, the lower the cash flow.

Last point: Higher leverage always means higher risk. In the low-leverage example, you have three cents in cash flow as a buffer against lower occupancies, lower rents or higher operating expenses. In the high-leverage example, unless you and/or the general partner are willing to put up some more money, you have no margin for error at all, no cushion if the property economics deteriorate. Higher leverage, higher risk.

Now, the purpose of this seemingly academic exercise is so you'll realize there are differences even among leveraged RELPs. If you have an account book full of people with fine earnings capacity, but who have an awful lot of trouble accumulating capital, your goal should be to pick a RELP that goes just for growth — one with high (70%-80%) leverage. If growth is the primary goal, but some current income and a higher level of safety are required as well, you'll look for a less aggressively leveraged RELP. You'll want to pick the one that approximates most closely the goals of your "natural market" and your client.

One cautionary note: Picking a highly leveraged RELP puts an added emphasis on finding a well-capitalized sponsor. That doesn't necessarily mean a larger sponsor, but size and strength can't possibly hurt. You need to see the sponsor's willingness and ability to use his deep pockets on behalf of partnerships he has sponsored. (When you're following this line of inquiry, plan to put a lot of distance between yourself and a wholesaler who says, "No sweat; we never have problem properties.")

PRESENTING THE CONCEPT

So now, for the buyer of growth, here's our first presentation of THE CONCEPT.

SUPERSTAR: *You know, you and I have very similar invest-
              ment goals. We've got to try to accumulate
              some serious capital, if we can. Isn't that one
              of your main financial goals?*

PROSPECT: *You bet it is.* (And the prospect is intrigued by
              your indentifying your objectives with his.)

SUPERSTAR: *Well, in the last year or so, I've gotten really
              interested in investment-grade real estate. I
              thought: Look, I help people choose invest-
              ments all day long, and I can't think of half a
              dozen things I've ever bought that outper-
              formed my own house. When I tried to figure
              out why, I saw that it was because I only put
              down a little equity, took a fair-sized mortgage,
              and sat back to watch the whole package rise
              in value. Same thing's happened to you, hasn't
              it?*

PROSPECT: (A BIG 10–4.)

SUPERSTAR: *The tax benefits of investing in real estate are
              very attractive, as well. You can deduct depre-
              ciation and end up with tax-free cash income
              like municipal bonds. I need all the help I can
              get in this area, too.*
                 *But I knew I wasn't cut out to be a free-lance
              property manager. I mean, I had no picture of
              myself investing in real estate other than through
              some real professionals. Do you?*

PROSPECT: *Not a chance. I can just about change my own
              light bulbs.*

SUPERSTAR: *So I started looking into what relationships my
              firm had with established, solid real estate oper-
              ators — people who look to investors like us
              for capital. And I found a really interesting
              partnership* (Optional — only if true: *and I've*

> *been accumulating it whenever I get the chance.) Want to hear about it?*

PROSPECT: *I sure would.*

(Speaking time: 1–1/2 minutes tops.)

Let's take a time-out and look at what went on in those 90 seconds.

First of all, you didn't try to pass yourself off as THE EXPERT. Far from it; in fact, you may even feel this presentation goes too far in the other direction. The point here was to show you how very simply, comfortably and conceptually you could pull up alongside somebody in your "natural market" and lay the concept of leveraged equity real estate partnerships on him in a totally nontechnical, nonthreatening way. This presentation makes absolutely no pretense to a lot of knowledge of real estate and none about taxation.

The presentation says you just started looking at RELPs a short while ago. You checked with your firm to see if they could recommend a good one. You bought some, and maybe your client would like to have a look. That's all. Who can get mad at you for that? Nobody. And, in fact, when you've opened in a low-key, conversational way like that, very few people will ever say, "No, I don't want to hear about it."

The "I'm-not-the-expert-all-I-do-is-love-this-thing" approach also tends to limit the prospect's inclination to hit you with a barrage of super-sharp questioning. He already senses that you like this investment because of the fit with your financial objectives and the recommendation by people in your firm who are paid to know about RELPs.

Come to think of it, what's wrong with that? If you called him with a common stock idea, would you shy away from telling your client that the research analyst who follows this company has picked half a dozen stocks that did really well over the last couple of years? And that you're really buying it because of his strong recommendation?

Well, for maybe the seventh time in this book, **why wouldn't you be comfortable doing the same things with RELPs you do with stocks?** Your client never asked you to be the expert. He asked you to work hard to find him good things to invest in. And isn't that exactly what you've just begun to do?

Sure it is. And in that minute and a half the client agreed with you *three different times* and then said "Yes" a fourth time when you asked him if he'd like to hear the story. You've implanted the basic concept (a professionally managed, investment-grade real estate portfolio stressing upside), and you haven't even named the product yet. You said: Here's something that I really like because it's good for people like you and me. (You have to be who you are, and you have to sell what you love.)

Perhaps you feel confident enough to come at the situation more strongly, and to take a more authoritative approach to your initial presentation. Fine. That's a commentary on your style, and on the way you see your relationship to your natural market. The same process is valid. Only the tone differs. The way you're going to say what you say will change. Try this on for size:

SUPERSTAR: *I imagine that we're both alike, in that our first source of capital growth investing is — directly or indirectly — common stocks. In the last couple of years, we've been well rewarded: The stock market's been a great place to be, hasn't it?*

PROSPECT: *Sure it has.* (Whether he's been in it or not is another question, but it's been great, and he knows it.)

SUPERSTAR: *After stock prices have had a historic run like this, though, it's hard to be as aggressive as you*

> *were even a year ago. That's not an attempt to predict the top; I just feel a lot more comfortable when stocks are nearer to their lows than to their highs. Don't you?*

PROSPECT: *I think so.* (If the truth be told, he loves it when everybody else is bullish, but he sees your point.)

SUPERSTAR: *Not only that, I think there are other assets with growth potential. Nothing beats the leverage in real estate for building capital, as you know from your own home. That's why I'd like you to take a look at diversifying into some investment-grade real estate. How does the concept sound to you?*

PROSPECT: *The concept sounds Ok. What have you got in mind?*

What do you suppose is the substantive difference between the two presentations? Right: There's *no* difference. There were some not-particularly-subtle stylistic variations, but that's about the size of it. One presentation had a kind of we're-all-in-the-same-boat-neighbor quality to it, while the other was a stronger statement about portfolio strategy. Neither is more right, except to the extent that your personal style or situation make one better.

The words don't matter. Here's the principle:

**CREATE ANY OPENING STATEMENT
THAT MANAGES TO SAY:
"I'VE BEEN THINKING ABOUT WHAT YOU NEED;
YOU NEED SIGNIFICANT CAPITAL GROWTH;
GOOD QUALITY REAL ESTATE ACCOMPLISHES THIS
GOAL FOR YOU."**

That's really all you want to do — providing, of course,

you give the person you're talking to ample opportunity to agree with you as you go along.

All that matters is that you generate, with empathy, a shared perception of financial need and a general notion that real estate (in this case, leveraged equity) fills that need.

Empathy, incidentally, is probably the single most critical element in building a highly relationship-oriented RELP practice. That's true if for no other reason than that you are going to ask for a lot of referrals from RELP investors. And people don't give referrals to someone they don't really like.

In the literature of sales and human relationships, it is said that you'll always give people one of two impressions: "This person really cares about me," or "This person is trying to sell me something." You decide which impression you really want to give, and the empathy factor will take care of itself. You needn't ooze all over people. Don't worry: They feel empathy when it's there, as well as when it's not.

GETTING TO THE SPECIFIC RELP

So now you're through your conceptual opening statement on leveraged RELPs, and your client has indicated a willingness to sit still long enough to hear a specific recommendation. What's the way into the particular RELP you have selected?

> *"My company has an excellent relationship with a real estate operator called Brixnstix Realty Company. I suppose we could do business with any property company we chose to, but we're just very comfortable with Brixnstix because . . ."*

(Using three very concise statements,
you plug in three points
that distinguish your sponsor.)

Examples:

(a) *they operate half a billion dollars worth of investment-grade real estate;*

(b) *their principals have been working successfully together for twenty years;*

(c) *they specialize in acquiring* (fill in the type of property or their major investment concept) *which we think is where you ought to be;*

(d) *they have a history of doing well for our clients;*

(e) *they know how to manage property aggressively, but they're financially very conservative;*

(f) *they know how to buy undermanaged property and turn it around;*

(g) *they've never lost a property in foreclosure, even when it took their own money to turn it around;*

(h) *they operate nationwide, and so they see a lot of diversified opportunities;*

(i) *we meet with the management regularly, and they go out of their way to keep us fully informed;*

(j) *they always seem to be able to spot rapidly growing markets;*

(k) *they really know Georgia and Alabama, and they stick with their success;*

(l) (any other one-line point about this sponsor that you really like.)

Now take another quick time-out, and look what you've accomplished. Point One of your five-point presentation was THE CONCEPT. Point Two is the general partner. Please look at the terms in which the general partner was presented, and try to feel the effect of the key, highlighted words and phrases:

CONSTANTS

- *My company* has an *excellent relationship* with . . .

MESSAGE: I'm not flying solo here. This investment was carefully selected. And we're happily married to these people for the long pull.

- . . . a real estate *operator* . . .

MESSAGE: This isn't just a syndicator, who adds an incremental layer of fees for no incremental value. These are operators. They provide the real estate savvy, we provide the capital.

- . . . we could do business with *any* . . .

MESSAGE: There were many beautiful ladies at the party. This is the one we **really** wanted to dance with.

- . . . but we're just *very comfortable* . . .

MESSAGE: Relax. When you get used to this, you'll really like it.

VARIABLES

- . . . operate *half a billion* dollars . . .

MESSAGE: Substance. (Incidentally, when discussing magnitudes, always talk debt and equity combined.)

- . . . a *history* of *doing well* for *our* clients . . .

MESSAGE: They do well. Never mind the details. And we know they do well, not because we read it someplace, but because our clients have profited.

- . . . *manage* property *aggressively* . . . *financially* very **conservative.**

MESSAGE: They'll work hard to produce for you, but they won't take unnecessary risks.

- . . . *undermanaged* property . . . *turn it around* . . .

MESSAGE: This isn't another big, dumb, blind pool. There's a real business strategy at work here.

When you get the hang of this, you can see why certain words and phrases work. They look very conversational and descriptive in a low-key way, but they turn out to be very forceful statements of your belief in this RELP's distinctive capabilities. So start thinking about the things you're really struck by in your RELP, and practice developing your three phrases. (Remember the way you say what you say is more important than what you say.)

Now back to the presentation.

"Their latest venture with us is a partnership that will raise $50 million in investor equity, and use another $100 million or so in mortgages, and buy perhaps 8 or 10 high quality, investment-grade properties. (Here you can say something specific about property types or geographical locations if it's appropriate. But do it quickly.)

It may take them six months or more to get the portfolio assembled, because they really like to take time to do a lot of screening and pick a small handful of opportunities. But when the process is complete, I believe you'll own as fine a real estate portfolio as any investor in this country. And I know you'll be a partner of some of the best property managers we've ever found.

The object of this investment is just one thing: maximizing the long-term growth potential of your real estate over the six to nine years of this partnership's life. That's what these people do best.

Don't look for a lot of current income, though, because real estate is like any other investment: It'll offer you a lot of growth, or a lot of current income, but not both. And, by the way, don't consider this or any other real estate investment with money you're probably going to need real soon. Real estate is a great long-term growth vehicle, not an in-and-outer.

Considering all that, what do you think is an appropriate amount for you to start with?"

If you go back now, and read the presentation straight through (picking any three of the suggested general partner sales bullets) you'll find:

YOUR SPEAKING TIME, AFTER THE CONCEPT, SHOULD BE UNDER THREE MINUTES.

Your total speaking time, start to finish, is less than *five minutes* (because, remember, THE CONCEPT took about a minute and a half). But in those five short minutes, look at all you accomplished:

(1) You identified a real investment goal. Also, you helped the client see how real estate can do what he needs done.

(2) You introduced your client to a superior general partner and mentioned *three* of that general partner's most interesting attributes.

(3) You identified a specific investment, and told your client
   (a) how big the partnership would be;
   (b) the relationship of equity to debt; and
   (c) about how many properties would be in the portfolio.

(4) You told him clearly what the investment objective was and the timing.

(5) You told him one benefit (current income) the investment *can't* provide, which is one approach to discussing risk.

Five basic points, in just about as many minutes. That's what it's all about.

No jargon. No complicated investment strategies. No convoluted financing terms. No numbers you can't prove. No estimates of how much money he'll make. No promises you might someday wish you had back. No hype. No sweat.

One more thing this very economical, low-key presentation style does is that you:

ALWAYS PRESUME ACCEPTANCE.

Right up to and including the very last line. You may have noticed, you ask him not whether he'd like to own this RELP, but how much he feels is right for him.

Does your client still have a hundred questions? Great. Your attitude should be: "If he thinks the stuff I told him in the presentation was great, wait 'til he hears the terrific answers to all his tough questions." Not that you know all the answers, of course; we already warranted to you that you don't. But you've gone in with the attitude that all the tough questions have great answers. (As promised, in Chapter 14 we'll show you a great way to get the answers, *right before your client's very eyes*.) Knowing lots of great answers is not the point.

The point, and it's one of the hardest things for less experienced RELP salespeople to accept, is that:

NO MATTER HOW MUCH LONGER YOU TALK AND HOW MANY MORE THINGS YOU SAY, YOUR CHANCES OF NAILING YOUR CLIENT'S DEEPEST FEARS DON'T EXIST.

You can't talk past people's real concerns; you have to let people verbalize them. So why postpone it? Make your best, simplest, most confident, most deeply-felt presentation, ask for an order, and then *shut up*.

Short, generic, presumptive presentations speak of nothing but confidence. RELPs are the ultimate confidence sale. Long,

detailed, technically specific, numbers-oriented presentations speak of nothing but fear. People do not invest their
confidence in frightened salespeople.

Please see that what we were doing in the last section was
building THE PRESENTATION. Leveraged equity RELPs —
the first of five basic RELP types we will cover — were just
used to show you how it's done. Put another way, THE
PRESENTATION was the body; leveraged equity is just one
of five suits (or dresses) we'll try on, and tailor to fit, that
body. The recommended RELP form may change but THE
PRESENTATION is THE PRESENTATION.

SUMMARY

- Simplify your presentations for the sake of your clients, not for you.

- Leveraged equity is the cornerstone RELP investment, if only because everybody's already done it at least once.

- Upside potential and risk are directly related to the amount of leverage you use; cash flow is inversely related to leverage.

- High-leverage RELP investing demands a deep-pocketed sponsor.

- The words don't matter. Empathy matters.

- A five-point presentation can be an infinitely adaptable form. Any RELP, and any salesperson's style, can be fitted to it.

- You've got five minutes. That's all. No matter how much longer you talk, or how much more you say, your chances of nailing the client's deepest fears don't exist.

11

How to Present
Unleveraged Equity RELPS

Let's see how to fit the unleveraged (or all-cash) equity RELP to THE PRESENTATION. First, what does an all-cash RELP look like? Cast your mind back to our brief discussion of how leverage affects upside cash flow and risk. The more leverage you use, the higher the upside and the risk, but the lower the cash flow. Suppose you take the leverage down to zero. What do you get?

(1) Less upside from appreciation on equity but more current cash flow which can grow. With no mortgage to feed, every dollar of rent above the operating expenses falls right to the bottom line.
(2) Competitive current return and some taxable income, because depreciation will not shelter all the cash flow.
(3) Low risk. What's the doomsday risk in real estate, anyway? Mortgage foreclosure. No mortgage, no foreclosure risk.

This description is the configuration of an all-cash RELP in a nutshell. So who would want this package of benefits? Who, in other words, would:

• be very hungry for current income and wouldn't care that some of it's taxable?

- be so risk-averse that the only risk they can stand is no risk at all?
- still need real inflation protection, because you can't trust bonds to hold purchasing power?
- be in for the long haul?

You guessed it: retirement plans, that's who. From $2,000 IRAs, to $7,500 KEOGHs, to $10-million pension plans, people look at all-cash RELPs and fall in love. Now there is a concept so simple and beautiful that everyone can understand it. No moving parts, batteries are included, and there's no assembly required. Indeed, the all-cash RELP is like Sara Lee: Nobody doesn't like it.

It helped that, when all-cash RELPs were introduced around 1980, pension trustees all over the country were watching their bond portfolios turn into wallpaper. They were very susceptible to an investment that generated reasonable current income *and* preserved the real (net of inflation) value of capital. That's the basic attraction of the all-cash RELP, as a bond alternative or a classic hedge against a fixed income portfolio.

Let's say that again, because it's the key to your selling efforts in all-cash RELPs, and will therefore become an essential conceptual building block of our generic presentation:

AN ALL-CASH RELP
IS A BOND (OR CD) ALTERNATIVE.

Retirement plans of every description are huge consumers of corporates, governments and CDs. And that makes a great deal of sense, based on their relative safety. The other attraction of debt is the ability of the pension plan to compound, on a tax-deferred basis, the current income which debt produces.

But, you have to be conscious of the essential limitations of debt securities. One problem is that they maintain your principal in dollars, not in purchasing power. Another is that when interest rates rise, the market price of bonds falls. If you hold bonds to maturity, fine: You'll get your (dollar-denominated) principal back. If you sell before maturity, you may take losses. Neither of these limitations makes debt a bad investment. But real estate may be able to cure the weaknesses of bonds. Here's how.

In Chapter 3 we pointed out that property value is essentially driven by cash flow. Cash flow, in turn, is a function of rents. And rents, sooner or later, respond directly to inflation. (If you aren't completely convinced that's true, or you don't remember how it works, please stop here. Go back, and read those sections again.) The message, of course, is that real estate ownership is one way for a retirement plan to plug into something whose capital value will stay pretty directly hooked into inflation, regardless of how great (or how little) inflation may be.

So, in presenting an all-cash RELP, you are offering your retirement plan client (or, for that matter, any low tax bracket investor) a safety valve. Not only are you showing him a solution to problems that debt securities don't answer, but you may also be protecting some part of his assets from the day when, as they inevitably will, interest rates cycle back up again. In the back of your mind, you also have the conviction that, **in any intermediate-term holding period, real estate will outperform bonds and CDs and is ideal for the part of your portfolio that doesn't demand liquidity.**

Permit a small digression at this point. Knowing the fundamentals of all-cash RELPs may also lead you to another market for them. Particularly when interest rates are low, all-cash real estate may be a great hedge in a sizable portfolio that's very heavily weighted toward intermediate-term tax-exempt bonds. If rates rise, whether just because of the inevitable cycle or due to inflation, the bonds will suffer, but the real estate will benefit.

THE PRESENTATION

So let's look at THE PRESENTATION for the all-cash RELP. We'll use, for our generic purpose, a RELP that's going to buy existing properties for cash. (Selling a new construction, all-cash RELP is a slightly different process, since you have to overcome two extra anxieties. One is the perception of the incremental risk of building versus buying. The other is the longer wait until cash flow from rents builds up. There's a great answer, of course: In the end, you can make a lot more money developing good real estate than you do buying proven properties. If you didn't, who'd bother taking the development risk?)

We're going to go back now to the presentation formula, with its five basic points:

(1) THE CONCEPT;
(2) The General Partner, with three specific attributes;
(3) The RELP itself;
(4) Investment objectives revisited; and
(5) Risks/Limitations.

In the presentation that follows, we stress the intrinsic merit of all-cash. (If you're interested in the "comparative approach," using all-cash as a bond alternative, see Chapter 1, where we used it to introduce you to THE CONCEPT.) This style is designed to be a very direct and forceful statement of the all-cash RELP.

It's also designed, as we think you'll see, to make the pension client say, "I think I can do better in bonds." And, later on in Chapter 13, we'll show you how to handle that objection. For the time being, just focus on this very gutsy superstar tactic: making a presentation that almost has to provoke an objection which you're quite prepared to annihilate.

This lets the superstar make a very positive, upbeat presentation. And it makes him look even better when he effortlessly KO's the first big objection without appearing to have moved his hands. Are you starting to like this?

Here's the approach:

SUPERSTAR: *Mr. IRA/Pension Prospect, I find that successful retirement-plan investing is one of the biggest challenges my clients and I face. That's because, over a long period of time, economic trends change so many times. Interest rates go up and down, inflation heats up and then cools off again, and the stock market . . . well, it behaves like the stock market always does. I think that makes retirement investing really difficult, don't you?*

PROSPECT: *You can say that again . . . twice!*

SUPERSTAR: *The one great long-term investment that seems to work well in all sorts of economic situations, though, is real estate. In periods of low interest rates and low inflation, like now, real estate's cash flow looks very good compared to just about anything else. And, if inflation heats up again, real estate works extremely well as an inflation hedge.*

I recommend owning some real estate in any retirement portfolio, just as I do in my own (say this only if true). Property that you buy for all-cash . . . that is, without mortgages . . . is probably the safest real estate investment you can make, and you get a lot of current income because you have no mortgage to pay. Does that concept make sense?

PROSPECT: *Well, I guess so. What specifically do you have in mind?*

(This recitation of THE CONCEPT just hits the high points. It doesn't give him much to hang his hat on, but it doesn't give him anything to shoot at, either. And it takes . . . you guessed it . . . A MINUTE AND A HALF!)

SUPERSTAR: *My firm has an excellent relationship with a real estate operator called Brixnstix Realty Company. I suppose we could do business with any property company we chose to, but we're just very comfortable with Brixnstix, because . . .*

   . . . they operate half a billion dollars worth of investment-grade real estate . . .

   . . . they really know _____ (fill in the blank with an area of the country, type of property or more general concept, like how to recognize value in strong markets as well as overbuilt ones) . . .

   . . . and they love to buy real estate for cash. I've often heard them say that there's nothing like negotiating with a seller when you've put a box of money on the table.

Any of that sound familiar to you? Ok. Now you are starting to see what we meant about the basic presentation being universal, so that it can comfortably wear whichever RELP type you drape over it.

And did you see how you began with your company's relationship with Brixnstix and ended by talking about your own relationship ("I've often heard them say . . . ")? Also, you used a very graphic image of the seller sitting there and not being able to take his eyes off the box of cash. That idea is going to hit home with any business person. **Tone.**

SUPERSTAR: *Our latest venture with them is a $50-million all-equity partnership which will own perhaps*

> *four or five important, investment-grade prop-*
> *erties. (Again, make a quick statement about*
> *property types and locations if it's appropriate.)*
> *It may take them six months or more to get*
> *that portfolio assembled, because they really*
> *like to take their time, do a lot of screening,*
> *and pick a small handful of opportunities.*

If you didn't recognize the purpose of the last statement the first time you saw it go by, we hope you got it this time. The reference to timing is to defuse the issue of when, during the relatively long offering period of a public RELP, the prospect should invest. The message is, "Come on, get aboard. This is a painstaking and professional process. Watch it unfold from a comfortable seat. Don't second-guess the engineer by trying to figure out when it will slow down long enough for you to jump on." Most RELPs do pay pre-formation interest at money market rates, so where's the percentage in being cute?

SUPERSTAR: *But when that process is complete, I believe*
you'll own as fine a real estate portfolio as any
pension investor in this country. And I know
you'll be a partner of some of the best property
managers we've ever found.

The investment goals of this partnership are
really the three most important things all my
pension clients say they're looking for:

(1) SAFETY. With no mortgage, there's no risk
of foreclosure, period. Nobody can ever
come and take your property away.

(2) INCOME. All-cash real estate maximizes
cash flow, again because there's no mort-
gage to pay off every month. Brixnstix's
properties typically break even at around

30% occupancy, and every additional dollar of rent becomes cash flow to you. Look for this partnership to start producing cash in the range of 6% a year, and expect that cash flow will increase at about the same rate as rents go up.

(3) CAPITAL APPRECIATION. Since good real estate trades on its cash yield, you can expect that your property values will move ahead pretty much in lock-step with rents and cash flows. And that's super-important to a retirement plan.

Now, there are limits to what this kind of real estate investing can do, of course. You can't hit an out-of-the park home run the way you can in highly leveraged real estate . . . your home, for instance. But, of course, you haven't got foreclosure risk, either.

Also, there's no guarantee that rents and cash flows will go up, even though, over a six to nine year holding period like this RELP's, they always have. But, again, that's a risk of the return on your money, not the return of your money.

Considering all this, what do you think is an appropriate percentage of your plan's assets to have in real estate?

Speaking time? That's right: three minutes. Nice, workman-like presentation. And, in the process, you shot two major objections out of the saddle before they could go for their guns.

One is that all-cash RELPs are pretty tame compared to people's expectations of real estate returns (which are really derived from leveraged real estate investing). A nontaxable investor earns an IRR in the 12%-15% range from an all-cash

RELP if rents go up 7% a year. Handsome returns compared to bonds, but not the kind of shoot-the-lights-out numbers a leveraged real estate investor looks for.

Second, the all-cash RELP investor doesn't know how much his cash flow will be every year (the way he knows the coupon of a bond, or the rate on a CD) because it's tied to rents, and you can't predict rent increases. Nothing can make this concern evaporate, *other than the fact that rents always go up over time.* And you made sure you pushed that button first.

You always want to be the one to touch on the risks and limitations of any partnership in the closing minute of your five-point presentation. It makes you look reasonable and even-handed. And when you're doing it right, you are going to neutralize one or two major objections before they come into play.

Our discussion of how to present public equity RELPs is now complete. We chose to spend all our time at either end of the leverage spectrum, in order to show that the same generic presentation formula can work with diametrically opposed RELP types. You have enough of the hang of it by now to go back and create your own presentation of a low-leverage RELP, one that's somewhere in between the two we concentrated on.

You must create THE PRESENTATION yourself. Ours is like a compass pointing the way. You need to draw your own road map. We suggest you try it before you move on to the next hurdle. Chapter 12 will show how to present RELPs that invest in mortgages.

SUMMARY

- All-cash real estate is a classically simple and beautiful way to own property.

- The benefits, current income, growth and low risk, are ideally suited for retirement plans.

- Unleveraged RELPs are bond substitutes that hedge the two risks in bonds — the interest rate cycle and inflation.

- Waiting for the bad guy to draw first went out with the Lone Ranger. You know what the big, common objections are: Use your presentation to shoot a couple of 'em right between the eyes.

12

How to Present Mortgage Loan RELPs, FREITs and MLPs

Will Rogers said that he wasn't nearly as concerned about the return on his money as he was about the return of his money.

And, indeed, the primary motives of most investors with respect to most of their capital are, and always will be:

SAFETY AND INCOME.

Nothing particularly earth-shaking in that revelation, is there? Of course not. But, there certainly is something new — and potentially very rewarding — in today's real estate solutions to the never-ending investor demand for instruments that may accomplish those two goals.

"Income" is easier to sell than "growth," too, not just because there's a bigger market for it, but *because you can usually quote a yield.* An investor isn't required to have as high a tolerance for ambiguity as "growth" demands and, in fact, the "income" investor usually has a fairly low threshold of confusion and anxiety. Behind everything labeled "opportunity," he sees a risk waiting to jump out and bite him on the neck. Whether physically or just emotionally, he's too old to believe in opportunity. He wants to know that he's not going to lose his capital and that he's going to earn a certain return. And then, he doesn't want to think about it any more.

The virtue of simplicity in your sales approach to RELPs was a matter of the utmost importance in discussing equity partnerships. **Simplicity literally becomes a matter of life and death when you start talking about income RELPs.**

And how could it not be? Look at what you're competing with: bonds and CDs. Every income investor over the age of 12 thinks he knows all the variables in those two types of investments, and he knows you can cover all of them inside of a minute. Yield, maturity, rating, FDIC insurance, and do you or don't you get a toaster when you buy one. That's about the extent of it. Do you think you're ever going to be able to explain to that mentality what a wraparound mortgage is? Good luck.

Where, then, is the high ground? What fixed point of reference can you stand on in your income-RELP sales effort, from which you can never be dislodged? What position can never be overcome by any combination of objections? You guessed it:

**REAL ESTATE ALWAYS OUTPERFORMS
BONDS, CDs, AND ANY OTHER
INCOME VEHICLE YOU CARE TO NAME.
IT HAS TO: IT ISN'T LIQUID.**

Now, perhaps, you see why we were at such seemingly academic pains, back in Chapter 3, to develop the conviction that, on the pure issue of illiquidity, real estate has to beat everything else in the game. This fact is the ultimate objection-killer.

That's not to say that you can't sell income RELPs unless you operate from this essential conviction. But without it, you'll work at least twice as hard for half the sales results, at best.

It's also, day in and day out, the ultimate qualifier of whether your prospect is ever going to buy an income-RELP or not. And the test only takes a few moments to administer. Just say this to every person you know who invests for income:

"You probably have a very nicely diversified portfolio of income-producing investments. You've got some bonds, some CDs, (perhaps) some dividend-paying common stocks, and maybe even a deferred annuity.

But tell me: do you own any mortgages?"

This style of inquiry will usually result in an answer that combines "No" and "What do you mean?" Even if it's just "No," come back with the same script:

"Investing in mortgages makes you a secured lender on income-producing real estate.

The income from mortgages is usually quite a bit more than from bonds, CDs or stocks . . . just think about the spread between the rate your own bank charges for a home mortgage, and the rate it pays on a CD.

When you think about it, real estate mortgages have to yield more than traditional investments because real estate isn't as readily liquid as, say, bonds or stocks.

But you have the comfort of knowing that your investment is secured by the real estate that you're lending on. In other words, if your borrowers don't pay what they owe you, you own their real estate.

(Here's an optional tag, if you want to start with a participating mortgage RELP: There are even ways of making mortgage loans that give you a piece of the appreciation in the real estate, in addition to the income and security.)

My firm has a particularly attractive way for our clients to invest in mortgages. Would you like to hear about it?"

Did you recognize that whole script for what it is? On its lowest-common-denominator, entry-level, start-from-a-standing-stop basis, you've just read . . . THE CONCEPT. And if you go back and read it out loud from the top, how long will it take? Right again: a minute and a half.

You can use this opening to start talking with *any* income investor about *any* mortgage RELP you like. (If you put in the optional section, you can even introduce the issue of equity participation.) And you have an infinitely adaptable, jargon-free, all-purpose way of qualifying an individual mortgage RELP prospect.

But, of course, the individual-investor market, important as it is, is completely dwarfed by the market for mortgage partnerships in qualified retirement plans. Why? For one simple reason: The income from a mortgage is taxable. So a tax-deferred retirement plan enjoys a two-fold extra benefit. First, the yield on mortgages is priced to compete with other *taxable* instruments, but the retirement plan doesn't pay taxes on it. Second, you're able to compound higher current earnings on a tax-deferred basis. (As we've observed earlier, compounding is what retirement investing is really all about.)

And, of course, you have an extra leg up in showing mortgage RELPs to retirement plans. The investors (or their trustees) tend not to have liquidity anxiety. Most of the money in the plan needn't be touched for a good long time. So, trading off some liquidity to get a higher return suits them just fine.

Presenting THE CONCEPT to everyone from an IRA inves-tor to the trustee of an important pension plan can be easy, if you couch your approach in terms of "success by associ-ation."

> *"You know, in uncertain economic times like these, you can pick up a lot from watching how the largest, most sophisticated institutions invest their assets.*
> *And what do banks, insurance companies and large pension plans do with the funds people entrust to them?*

EXACTLY . . . They lend money on real estate, in the form of mortgages. Mortgage lending is a very attractive investment medium for them, for two reasons.

First, they get a lot higher return on mortgages than they do from bonds or income stocks. They demand higher returns because real estate isn't as readily liquid as other investments.

Second, they know mortgages are secured by the real estate properties they lend on. And if the borrowers are in trouble, the lending institution takes the property.

(Again, add this only if you're leaning toward a participating mortgage RELP: There are even ways of making mortgage loans that give you a piece of the appreciation in the real estate, in addition to the income and security.)

These days, there are a number of good opportunities for your retirement plan to become a mortgage lender. Would you like to hear about one?"

Here again, just as you're beginning to discuss THE CONCEPT of mortgage lending, you can stake out the high ground and head off what may be the most common objection to real estate investing. Seize the "liquidity premium" idea before your presentation ever gets into second gear.

PRESENTING THE PEOPLE

When either your individual or your retirement plan prospect says, "Ok, tell me the story," then you're ready to go. Try your patented soliloquy about your firm's relationship with Brixnstix Realty Company, in exactly the words you used in presenting an equity RELP. That just stands to reason: You're trying to create the same level of confidence in the general partners and in your relationship with them that you were imparting earlier, and for the same reasons.

Reach the point where you roll out the three individual characteristics which, for you, make Brixnstix uniquely attractive. Only this time, you'll want to use at least one of them to highlight the sponsor's capabilities as a *lender*.

" . . . They've borrowed about $2 billion in mortgages on properties they've owned, so they know how to analyze mortgages from both sides . . . "

(or)

" . . . A true real estate operator knows how to get inside a property and really see what kind of loan it will support . . . "

The message is simply this: Whether you're presenting equity or debt doesn't matter. Everything we've said about the paramount importance of the general partner still goes. Take your time and build your prospect's confidence in the people you've chosen to manage the real estate portion of his invested capital. When he sees that your firm has done its homework, and that you believe in the people, then he'll feel he's being well looked after.

Mastering the intricacies of mortgage lending is not the point. A mortgage, or even a portfolio of mortgages, is a pretty abstract thing to the average investor. People will make an act of faith in other people, but not in pieces of paper.

AVOID MORTGAGE RELP GRIDLOCK

There are three basic types of mortgage funds, and both you and your clients probably already know a heck of a lot more about them than you think you do. The quickest way to unlock that common-sense understanding is to express the character of each different loan in its simplest terms.

Start with the certainty that there's an inverse relationship between the total return you can expect from a mortgage fund and its degree of safety. Want more safety? You can have it, but the cost will be a lower overall yield. The other inverse relationship you'll want to key on is the one between current yield and "participation." (Participation refers to earning part of the increases in rents and appreciation on sale.)

Sure, a lot of other variables affect the equation: loan-to-value ratios, property type, and others. For purposes of sales strategy, though, stay with these two for a while.

From these relationships, you can pretty easily build yourself a grid of the three major mortgage RELP types, and start moving comfortably around on it as you begin to sense what a client's true needs and risk tolerances are.

MORTGAGE LOAN RELP GRID			
RELP TYPE	SAFETY	CURRENT YIELD	EQUITY PARTICIPATION
Insured Mortgage Loan Funds	All you could want; they're buying federally insured mortgages at discounts from par or only lending a fraction of the value of the collateral.	Better than bonds.	None. Sure, the yield will be enhanced a little if the mortgages are paid off earlier than expected, but only the little old lady from Pasadena would feel like that was an equity kicker.
Participating First Mortgage Funds	Pretty good. Not federally insured, mind you, but you're probably not lending more than 75% to 80% of a property's value, and you hold the first lien on the real estate. So you can sleep OK.	Perhaps equal to bonds in the early years, but much higher later on.	Nothing to sneeze at, but no lifestyle changer, either. After all, you made a pretty safe loan, so you're not going to get a big box of upside.
Participating Second (or Wraparound) Mortgage Funds	Least secure of the three. You're probably loaning closer to the full value of the property, and if the real estate gets in trouble, the first mortgage holder gets all his money out before you get any.	Maybe just a tad less than a participating first mortgage, but can rise substantially after the first few years.	A big piece of the upside. Why? Because when you scratch 'n' sniff second debt, it feels an awful lot like equity. So it ought to be required to act like equity.

(We deliberately left noninsured, straight-rate debt funds out of the grid. They have a little less safety and a little more yield than insured funds. But, what the heck? We figured, if you're going to go for safety, might as well go all the way. Besides, three types are enough.)

Laying this grid out may arouse your suspicions. Perhaps we're encouraging you to learn all about the three types of, or even three specific, mortgage RELPs before you start a prospecting campaign. Not at all. Our basic thesis is still that you'll be better off finding one mortgage RELP that you really feel is an interesting and superior transaction. Then buy it in your IRA, or in your kids' trust accounts. And then, present it at least once every day.

The point of showing you the grid is to demonstrate fairly important ideas about mortgage RELPs. This new generation of debt RELPs is far from being the bewildering, undifferentiable blizzard it may appear to be. They can be easily understood as built around a very logical set of trade-offs among safety, current yield and upside. More important, once you see these trade-offs for what they are, you learn to easily and comfortably shift gears. Instead of losing a sale when a prospect says, "I need more income; I'm not concerned with building capital," or, "I'm not trying to squeeze the last dollar out of the yield; not losing the principal is my greatest concern," you learn to switch RELPs.

And that ability to adjust feels very professional, and very good, both to your prospects and to you.

THE THREE-PART FORMULA

Let's review the bidding now, and build some sales presentations.

At the beginning of this chapter, we established two very basic approaches to THE CONCEPT: one for individual investors and one for qualified plans. We tried to set two introductions up so that you wouldn't have to vary a word no matter what types of mortgage RELP you wanted to use.

Next, we were at some pains to encourage you to go carefully and completely through the whole set-up about the general partner you've chosen. You need to stress the attributes leading a reasonable observer to believe that Brixnstix does, indeed, have significant skills as a mortgage loan underwriter who can also step right in and manage a property that gets in trouble.

So, now it's time for the third part of our presentation formula, describing the partnership we're going to recommend. We'll try to give the client an idea of the returns we're looking for and the timing. Don't forget to make some allusion to the limitations and/or risks of this type of investing. Then, we'll do a trial close (undoubtedly a prelude to Q&A).

INSURED MORTGAGE FUNDS

These funds generally combine a very specific and easily explainable package of benefits. Let's review what they are, and then see how we want to explain them to an investor.

First, the fund will buy only mortgages that are insured by the Federal Housing Authority (FHA) or securities issued by the Government National Mortgage Association (GNMA). Older mortgages may have been made at interest rates measurably below today's market. The result: The mortgages are trading at a discount to the principal value.

How do you know that? Every few months, the U.S. Department of Housing and Urban Development (HUD) auctions off insured mortgages. Bidders purchase these mortgages, in effect marking them to the market. Mortgages carrying interest rates lower than today's rates trade at a discount.

For all practical purposes, insured mortgages don't have any more risk than Treasury bonds. That's because the folks who insure your investment also have a wholly-owned subsidiary called the U.S. Mint. As Bob and Ray have long pointed out, the Mint is America's leading producer of new money.

So, about the worst thing that's going to happen is that the mortgages will just limp along until maturity, effectively returning the rate you bargained for at the auction, together with your principal.

Beside the discount, another "angle" is that the people who assemble funds, or pools, of insured mortgages are trying to spot ones which have some chance of being paid off before the scheduled maturity. (Early pay-off increases the effective yield when you buy mortgages at a discount.) Some property is a good candidate for early pay-off of its mortgage. Managers look for well-located, well-maintained property old enough to have used up all its tax benefits, reasoning that it may be a good target for sale or maybe even condo conversion. They have a hunch things are moving this way now, as the federal government moves to unwind its involvement in the landlord business.

It's not any more complicated than that. You earn a fixed rate of return, government-guaranteed. Your return bumps if, in fact, some of the mortgages are paid before maturity.

How do we present the essentials to an investor? Well, first of all, here's how you *don't:* by telling him the mortgages are going to be paid off early. The whole theme of this book, in case you hadn't noticed, is:

UNDERSELL. UNDERSELL. UNDERSELL.

Never press — confident salespeople don't have to. The message is going to be: Prepayment, if it happens, will be a very nice icing on a perfectly delightful plain cake. But if the whole dessert turns out to be plain cake, and that's not enough for your prospect, he should be encouraged to look elsewhere on the menu.

Here's one way to do the third section of The Presentation.

"Their latest venture with us is something very different, very timely . . . and very much suited to today's interest rate environment, where investors like us find it harder and harder to capture the yields we need without compromising our demand for safety.

Brixnstix Federally Insured Mortgage Fund III will be a $50-million portfolio of existing mortgages with one very important thing in common: All the mortgages will be guaranteed by an agency of the federal government.

Typically, these mortgages will have been made some years ago, when mortgage rates were lower than they are now. So, the mortgages can be bought at less than their face value (add, if you know the investor understands this: the way bonds can). So you know you've got a locked-in, government-guaranteed yield.

You can look for a cash yield, paid quarterly, of around N% a year, which sure looks good to me when I consider today's CD rates, and the like.

But there's something else. You see, Brixnstix is looking for mortgages that may not go all the way to scheduled maturity . . . mortgages that may be prepaid because the underlying property is good real estate and might be sold or converted to condos before the mortgage expires.

After all, anyone with a good pocket calculator can tell you if a particular mortgage is priced right in terms of its current yield. But I trust an authentic real estate operator like Brixnstix to spot opportunities in the underlying property.

What could that be worth in terms of enhanced yield? Your guess is every bit as good as mine, and probably better. I just know that you'll have your going-in, government-guaranteed yield, and that any prepayments are just added benefits.

*Like any fixed-income security, there'll be some risk
that you won't get your full investment back if you want
to sell when interest rates are higher, but that's par for the
course. I wouldn't want you to consider this investment
with any money you're likely to need in a hurry, anyway.*

*Do you have any bonds or CDs maturing soon that will
need this kind of home?"*

Even in your slowest James Stewart drawl, you're going to
bring that presentation home in two minutes flat. And what
does it say? "Here's a good, safe, income investment. If you
hang on, it'll never get any worse than it is today, and with
good management and a couple of breaks, you might do a
good bit better." And the style is comforting, nonthreatening,
and as underselling as it can possibly be.

Does the client want more yield? Well, we can amble on
up the yield curve, all right, but not with this level of safety.
Was he waiting to pounce on you with the liquidity argument, or with the risk of an interest rate spike? No luck: You
dusted off those two issues yourself, in the last part of the
presentation.

Can you hear the underlying message? Whatever the configuration of the client's income need, you're perfectly confident you've got a sensible real estate solution for it. You
want to keep your presentation in a nice, low-key, "Let's try
this one on for size" kind of tone. In fact, the clothing analogy
is worth bringing up again here. You have your client in the
store, and you'll both keep looking, in a leisurely fashion,
until you find the garment that's just right.

This is not a situation where, if you don't pick exactly the
right suit/dress on the first try, your customer will leave in a
huff. Make your presentation with the unspoken conviction
that you are *inevitably* going to come up with the perfect fit
sooner or later. As with most things you're pretty sure will
happen, you'll find that you'll eventually be right. An insured
mortgage fund is a relatively riskless presentation. Why?

Because nobody can ever get mad at you for offering him something in which the federal government guarantees his investment. And because, as always:

WHEN THE PROSPECT TELLS YOU WHY HE WON'T BUY AN INSURED MORTGAGE FUND, HE HAS TOLD YOU WHAT HE WILL BUY.

PARTICIPATING FIRST MORTGAGE FUNDS

On virtually every page of this book, you are reminded that a great deal of the communication that takes place in the RELP sales process is nonverbal. We've encouraged you to try to develop ways of sending and receiving the deeper, more genuine attitudinal signals that are, we believe, the key to RELP superstardom. (And, in the next chapter on Questions & Answers, we'll be taking this perception to even higher levels.)

Here's a good example. If, during your quiet, laid-back, safety-oriented presentation of an insured RELP, you notice that your prospect has fallen asleep, you can be sure he's trying to tell you something. His nonverbal message to you is that, safe and simple and precise as your suggestion may be:

"It ain't no fun."

Participating mortgages are fun. Any (good) prospect can be induced to share even a little of your enthusiasm for having your cake and eating it too — which is the very essence of what a participating mortgage does for you.

Look here . . . what has always been the one absolutely terrible thing about being a traditional mortgage lender? You earn a fixed rate of return in dollars, not in purchasing power; and the developer, whose building you finance, walks away with *all the profits.*

And what's historically been the one absolutely terrible thing about being an owner of real estate? If you don't pay, the person holding your mortgage (who has no particular interest in the ups and downs of your business, and not much of a sense of humor, either) can always drop in, hand you a dollar and your mortgage note torn in half, and take away your building. Not the garage, not the bottom six floors — *the whole building.*

Now, what if you could somehow be, in most important respects, both a secured lender *and* a part owner of the real estate? Wouldn't that be pretty close to the best of both worlds?

The instrument through which you can effect this marvelous circumstance is called a participating mortgage. And it's about the most fun you can have selling real estate as an income investment.

Let's talk a little bit about the second of our three mortgage RELP types, the participating first mortgage fund. In most participating first mortgages, the lender is saying to the owner of the real estate, "I'm willing to put up the money at a fixed interest rate below the market, provided you'll give me a percentage of all the upside." ("Upside" refers to increases in rents or operating income and any appreciation in the property.) Be aware, though, that a first mortgage of, say, 75% of a property's value is, by most standards, a pretty safe loan. So the owner who accepts the participating loan isn't going to be willing to give up a big piece of the upside for only a slightly lower current interest cost.

Now comes the RELP superstar's opportunity. The investor in a participating first mortgage partnership isn't trying to put one out of the park in deep center field. He's trying to earn a good competitive current return, but knows that he doesn't want the inflation or interest rate risk of a strictly fixed-dollar return investment. (That description applies to nine out of ten intelligent pension fund managers in the U.S., among other people.)

The challenge, then, is just describing the partnership simply. Having enunciated THE CONCEPT, and having said grace over the general partner, you have to give your prospect a simple, clear idea of how a participating first mortgage RELP can lick its weight in wildcats . . . in just about two minutes. Here's our approach:

"Their latest venture with us is a $50-million partnership called Brixnstix Mortgage Investors VII. This program will be a secured first mortgage lender. In other words, Brixnstix will lend the partnership's capital on top quality, investment-grade real estate.

The loans they make will produce two things for the investors: A competitive current return and equity participation in the success of the real estate, both from increases in operating cash flow and from a share in the ultimate sale of the properties.

This special kind of mortgage investment gives you the best of both worlds in real estate.

First, you have the safety and regular income of the stated interest rate you receive on a mortgage . . . with the property itself as collateral on your loan.

Second, you have a share of increased rents (cash flow) and appreciation that good real estate can produce . . . but without the traditional equity ownership risk of foreclosure.

It may take Brixnstix the better part of six months to invest all of the investor's capital in this mortgage portfolio, because they really like to take their time and look for a few superior opportunities.

But when they're finished, I believe you'll own as fine a portfolio of mortgages as any (pension) investor in the country.

You'll be getting a quarterly income stream in the N% range. And you'll share in any profits from increasing rents, and from appreciation when your properties are sold or refinanced.

*Safety, income, and exposure to the prospect of increas-
ing capital values . . . those are the things my most
sophisticated individual (retirement) investors are looking
for these days. And I can't find anything that packages
those potential benefits the way Brixnstix Mortgage does.*

*Do you have any bonds or CDs maturing soon that will
need this kind of home?"*

In just this one presentation, the issue of risk is ignored. In
part, that's because the risk of first mortgage lending is fairly
obvious: The borrower doesn't pay, and you take back the
real estate. More importantly, **we'd prefer the prospect to ask
about the risk himself because the answer is such a beauty,**
and so simple: "If you are involved in a situation where you
have to take over and operate a troubled property, you'll
need the hands-on *operating experience* of Brixnstix to turn
the tide."

The discussion is steered right back to what you've
described all along as the central issue: the general partner.
And that neat loop back through a previously-covered presentation point gives you a perfect opportunity to try another
close. And you'll keep closing until you get it right. Sooner or
later, a reasonable prospect comes to see the beauty of
having it both ways with a participating mortgage. It takes a
really determined nonprospect not to love that.

PARTICIPATING SECOND MORTGAGE FUNDS

If a prospect can handle the risk, participating second
mortgage funds are conceptually a very exciting vehicle. (We
know what you cynics are saying: "Exciting mortgage" is a
phrase like "military intelligence" and "water landing" — a
contradiction in terms.)

Yes, exciting. When you think about it, **you basically only
get to put a second mortgage on a property which is already**

a proven winner. That's the very essence of second lending, and it isn't hard to see why.

Ten years ago, say, a developer built a shopping center in the middle of a potato field. Over the intervening decade, that area turned into the hottest new residential location in town. The shopping center cost $10 million to build, and was originally mortgaged for $8 million at a rate below today's mortgage rates. The property is now worth $18 million and the mortgage balance is paid down to $7 million.

The owner would love to pull some of the appreciated equity (unrealized gain) out of there and develop something else. But he doesn't want to sell, because he thinks the property still has a lot of room to run, and he doesn't particularly care to pay the tax on the gain. If he simply refinances, he will lose the advantage of the attractive low rate of interest on his original mortgage loan.

A second mortgage loan is just the ticket in this situation. Proceeds of loans are tax free to the borrower. But a traditional, straight-rate second might require interest, say, at a healthy premium to prime. A high interest rate means you can't borrow a lot because the property's cash flow has to cover the additional debt service.

But if the owner can convince a lender that this property will keep on prospering, maybe the lender will give up some current income for a participation in the cash flow and the appreciation. It's not unusual for participating second mortgage loans to have current yield approaching the prime rate. If so, current debt service will be that much lower, allowing greater leverage. There you have the gearworks of a participating second mortgage loan fund.

The risk, of course, is that after you put the second loan on the property, there's quite a bit of debt to carry in total. If cash flow heads south instead of north, default can occur. As the second lender, you'll have to step in, take control of the property, and still have the first mortgage lender to contend with.

That's why your second loan fund should be managed by a smart, aggressive and deep-pocketed sponsor. A proper general partner should be able to see the storm clouds gathering and be able to assume the active management of the property. That ability is what separates the real, hands-on real estate operator from a syndicator who's just reaching for extra yield by putting out risky loans.

The challenge, in constructing your third-stage, two-minute presentation of a participating second mortgage RELP, is to present its genuinely superior earnings potential without trimming on the issue of risk.

That's just a little bit harder than it sounds. Most salespeople know instinctively that people *say* they want safety and good income, but what they *mean* is that they want high income and the illusion of safety. And, you can sell second mortgage RELPs just by quoting the yield and the participation, assuring your prospects that they're becoming a "secured mortgage lender." But you shouldn't, and our model presentation doesn't.

> *"Our latest venture with them is a $50-million partnership called Brixnstix Income Fund XVIII. In this vehicle, Brixnstix looks for seasoned, successful properties on which to make second mortgages.*
>
> *Candidates for the fund will typically be shopping centers, office buildings and apartments that have two things in common: They were built a few years ago, and they've worked out real well.*
>
> *Now their value is up, the balance on the original mortgage is down, and the owners would love to pull some of the profit out . . . but they don't want to sell.*
>
> *That gives Brixnstix the opportunity to go in and offer a second mortgage on the property — a second mortgage*

that will offer you a competitive current return, but a loan that will also participate in all the future increases in the property's cash flow and increases in value, from here on out.

That makes great sense for the property owners. And it makes great sense for you as an investor who wants income, but wants his capital to be able to grow, as well.

Now, it may take Brixnstix the better part of six months to assemble this whole mortgage portfolio, because they really like to take their time and look for a few superior opportunities.

But when they're finished, I believe you'll own as fine a portfolio of mortgages as any (pension) investor in the country.

You'll be getting a quarterly income stream in the N% range. And you'll own a piece of any continuing increases in cash flow from rents and in the value of the property.

Now, second mortgage lending does produce a very dynamic overall return, relative to other "income" investments. And you are taking some added risk to get that return. Basically, the position of a second lender on a property is behind that of the first lender.

That's why it's of critical importance to look at this kind of investment only if it's managed by first-class, hands on real estate operators like Brixnstix, who have a proven record of managing property of this kind, and who are willing to subordinate their profit from this partnership to your receiving a competitive return first.

Do you have any bonds or CDs maturing soon that could use this kind of home?"

Second mortgage RELPs are a real way of investing for income *and* growth. The key is the fact that the added risk requires the general partner to be an experienced operator. You can't make a second loan RELP look as passive as a bond, nor should you try. So make 'em exciting.

REVIEW THE PRESENTATION MANUFACTURING SYSTEM

Those are the three major mortgage RELP types. Together with leveraged and all-cash equity partnerships, they constitute the five basic RELP types. In the first couple of years of your systematic RELP sales effort, you'll probably want to concentrate in just a couple of areas in which you find the deals that you love.

Please notice that Chapters 8 through 12 of this book use one consistent and unified theory of presentations. Before plunging ahead into the theory and practice of Q&A (which follows), you might just want to take a break, go back, and read these chapters through completely. Because the more clearly you see that this is a top-to-bottom system for manufacturing a simple, compelling, anxiety-free presentation of *any* RELP, the better off you'll be. When you find a new RELP that you'd really like people to own a lot of, you can plug in our presentation formula, and watch it shine.

FREITS AND REITS

Just before moving on, though, let's spend a little time on the sales aspects of some other real estate investments that are growing in popularity: finite-life real estate investment trusts (FREITs) and REITs.

Either of these entities can have a portfolio of all kinds of mortgages, as well as equity. So there's no such thing as one generic FREIT or REIT presentation. The correct presentation will be geared to the investment in the portfolio.

But there is something common that ought to be discussed. **REITs and FREITs are liquid.** The securities will trade over-the-counter, or on a stock exchange. (Some partnerships will be traded and be liquid. In this case, the limited partnership interests are replaced by a depositary receipt. Those receipts, or units, are traded.)

In presenting a traded security, simply layer into those last two minutes a sentence telling your prospect that his interest in the partnership will have a market value which may be up or down at any given time, but which will give him the opportunity to quote his investment, and to sell it if he needs to.

FREITs and REITs are interesting, too, because retirement plans can legally own leveraged real estate in them. Their cash distributions from leveraged properties aren't classed as "unrelated business taxable income." They might be just the ticket for an aggressive pension investor. The liquidity of FREITs and REITs appeals to the individual or retirement plan who wants to know that he can earn the traditional benefits of real estate, with an escape hatch of a market for the shares in a pinch.

MLPs

Another "liquid" real estate security that deserves discussion is the Master Limited Partnership (MLP). Once again, it's important to stress that the way you present the concept of the investment doesn't change. **Never let the form of the investment become the focus of your presentation.** The MLP form simply adds the benefit — and risk — of liquidity to the particular type of real estate you're looking at. (What risk, you ask? Why, the risk that the securities markets, in their wisdom, will drive the price of the MLP way down below its real asset value. Stranger things have happened.)

There are a couple of aspects of MLPs that make them potentially interesting. First, an MLP can conduct an active business — developing property, running hotels, operating nursing homes — in a way that a REIT can't. REITs (and FREITs) can only be passive investors.

Perhaps even more important (unless and until Congress or the Treasury gets around to "fixing" it) is the fact that MLPs produce (to the extent their cash flow is taxable) "passive" income, as defined by the 1986 Tax Reform Act. In other words, you can use the taxable income from an MLP (but not from a REIT or FREIT) to absorb "passive" losses from old tax shelters: losses which would otherwise go on circling the field for years without a place to land, because the investor hasn't got "passive" income.

Just remember that form follows function. What you're learning to do in this book is to show your clients good property, good management and the potential for a superior return. The box that those benefits come in can't matter *too* much.

SUMMARY

- Mortgage loan partnerships provide safety and income and therefore have a larger natural market than equity RELPs.

- The "high ground" of the mortgage RELP presentation is relative investment performance and the superior return because of illiquidity.

- Retirement plans are the natural market.

- The three types of mortgage RELPs can be easily distinguished by thinking of our old friends current return, risk and upside potential.

- While the investments they make and the benefits they offer can be similar to any one of the RELP types, REITs, FREITs and MLPs are different . . . they are liquid.

13

Questions & Answers I: Gaining the Upper Hand

The fear of being asked a question we can't answer is the single most paralyzing obstacle to movement up the RELP learning curve. Being embarrassed by repeated questions to which one doesn't know the answer (whether they come from the prospect or his CPA) is the primary cause of failure to complete a RELP prospecting program.

We've deliberately put off a discussion of answers to objections with respect to each individual RELP type. You don't need a chapter full of snappy retorts, put-downs and indications of moral superiority. **You need to know how to really answer objections, not how to bandy words.**

UNLOAD THE SMOKING GUN

In this chapter, we're going to develop the proper approach to handling Q&A — the philosophy, if you will. The first principle in this philosophy — the perception behind which you have to line up all your other perceptions — is:

THERE IS NO SMOKING GUN.

The possibility *does not exist* that your client, his CPA, or anyone else, can find the fatal flaw in your RELP — an aspect of the transaction that makes it objectively bad. This perception is a terribly hard thing for most would-be RELP superstars to accept. Yet acceptance of it is absolutely critical.

Look . . . you can't ever communicate perfect confidence in your product unless you believe totally in that product. If you're unconsciously tip-toeing through an emotional mine field of fear that your client will discover something that's *absolutely, intrinsically wrong* with your RELP, then:

YOU CANNOT SELL
BECAUSE YOU AREN'T REALLY SOLD.

This Q&A philosophy is not an encouragement to blind, unreasoning faith. Nor is it a suggestion that, if so many other smart salespeople accept a concept, you ought to accept it, too. (If the Petro-Lewis experience didn't teach us anything else, at least let it have taught us *that*.)

But it is a challenge to you. You have to have enough confidence in your firm's due diligence capability to believe that, if there were a smoking gun in the transaction, the firm would have found it. If you feel differently, (a) you'd better think about whether you really want to try to sell this stuff, and/or (b) you'd better start asking yourself whether you're working for the right firm.

Indeed, most RELP superstars know the answer whenever the prospect/CPA says, "I've found the aspect that makes this RELP an objectively bad deal." Instinctively and without a flicker of fear, they say, "No, you haven't." Anybody can voice an objection you can't immediately answer. Anybody can show you that this RELP isn't right for a particular investor. But, no one can tell you that this RELP is an objectively bad deal.

Do whatever it takes to get you to that confidence level. **Without that iron conviction, you will never attain RELP superstardom.** The RELP superstar never wavers in one certainty: Although there may be an infinite number of detailed questions to which he doesn't know the answer, **the super-star is always in possession of the essential truth that his is a superior RELP.**

STATED VERSUS REAL OBJECTIONS

The second principle in this philosophy is:

THE PROSPECT'S STATED QUESTION OR OBJECTION IS NOT, IN FACT, HIS REAL QUESTION OR OBJECTION.

Take just as much time as you need, and roll that one around in your head very slowly. To the cynical observer, this statement may appear to be saying that the prospect is engaged in trying to head-fake you, and deliberately raising "red herrings" in order to hide his real objections from you. But if you're *sincerely* prospecting people who are *sincerely* trying to understand your recommendations, you won't end up talking at length with prospects who are playing mind games with you. (As we've observed before, if you're qualifying your prospects well, this shouldn't be a major problem.)

How, then, do we explain our statement that the prospect is usually not voicing the question/objection he really means? It's simple. Remember, as we've insisted throughout this book, that the prospect simply does not have the frame of reference for the business of real estate that he does for securities investments.

If you had called him with a recommendation to buy the common stock of Winnebago Industries (the motor home/RV manufacturer), you and he would have a shared perception of the relevant issues. Suppose your research department feels that Winnebago is a great buy because: (1) oil is down for the count, and sales of motor homes take off when fuel costs are low; and (2) as the population ages and retires, motor homes become a favorite way for older folks to do all the traveling they've been wanting to do all these years.

Your client may well disagree. He may feel that oil is at an exaggerated cyclical low, and that the depression in drilling is just setting up the next oil "shock." Moreover, he may say that the vicious and prolonged airline "fare wars" mean that people can fly wherever their fancy takes them (just as cheaply and far more conveniently).

But at least you agree to disagree on a common understanding of the central issues.

You can't presume that common understanding in real estate. In fact, you're safe to assume just the opposite: that the prospect can't have completely thought out the point he's raising. After all, he hasn't enough previous experience to guide him.

The truth of this observation puts an entirely new light on the question and objections handling process in a RELP sales situation. Instead of the terrible weight of the obligation to answer, crisply and correctly, every question your prospect can conjure up out of thin air, your attitude shifts to the perception that:

"I don't think he understands what he asked me."

This is usually a stunning revelation to the RELP superstar-in-training. But it shouldn't come as a shock. From the very first few minutes you were reading this book, and in every subsequent chapter, we have been at great pains to bring home to you the absolute certainty that your prospect does not understand RELPs in the same familiar way that he understands so many other investments you discuss with him. And you must have accepted that notion to some degree, because you're still, over a hundred pages later, reading this book.

For instance, back in the section on how to present an all-cash RELP, we said that one style of making this kind of presentation automatically provokes the objection: "I can do better in bonds." The way we did that was to make a presentation entirely devoid of numbers except for one statement: that "cash flow should start in the range of 6%." (If the statement does not provoke the bond preference objection, for heaven's sake reach over and check the prospect's pulse.)

When you read it, you may have grinned to yourself and said, "I remember the answer to that! First, real estate always outperforms bonds over any intermediate-term holding period. And second, real estate would have to outperform liquid investments like bonds, or nobody would buy it." And, indeed, those are extremely logical and compelling answers to the *stated* objection.

But that's not the right answer because:

**THERE IS ABSOLUTELY NO REASON TO
SUPPOSE THAT A QUESTION OR OBJECTION,
AS STATED,
HAS ANYTHING TO DO WITH WHAT'S REALLY
BOTHERING THE PROSPECT.**

The correct answer to the objection, "I can do better in bonds," is, of course, "I hope so."

What's that? You don't see why that's the right answer? Exactly. Now you see why we held our fire on Q&A, and why we're devoting two whole chapters to it.

To become a successful RELP superstar, you have to have a complete, built-from-the-ground-up philosophy of handling questions and objections. That philosophy, like everything else in this book, must be rooted in an appreciation of the real emotions and feelings of your prospects and in your response to them. It can't be derived from facts or numbers. (In the meantime, if the suspense of why "I hope so" is the right answer to the bond objection is killing you, please stay tuned. ''All,'' as Agatha Christie's Hercule Poirot always says when he's assembling the suspects in the drawing room, ''will be revealed.'')

U-TURN THE QUESTIONS AROUND

Let's review the bidding. First, the prospect doesn't have much, if any, conceptual feeling for RELPs. Second, the presentation you made focused completely on the big picture, to the exclusion of a great wealth of detail. And, finally, you tried to close by asking the prospect for the dollar amount of the commitment he thought was appropriate . . . which had to make him snap out any half-baked question or objection that popped into his mind. Now, when a question comes tumbling out of his mouth, why on earth would you take it seriously?

Right: you wouldn't. Instead, you'd sit back, relax, and, in a sincere attempt to make your prospect examine what his own question/objection means, either:

GIVE A NON-ANSWER ANSWER
OR ANSWER THE QUESTION WITH A QUESTION.

Hear are two examples:

ANSWER WITH A NON-ANSWER

PROSPECT: *I can do better in bonds.*

SUPERSTAR: *I hope so.*

ANSWER WITH A QUESTION

PROSPECT: *What if I get audited?*

SUPERSTAR: *What if you do?*

The first response is a non-answer answer. The second is answering a question with a question. Incidentally, **after responding in either one of these two ways, you always wait five full seconds before you say anything else.** This pause lets the clear understanding sink into the prospect's consciousness that his challenge has not disturbed you.

And you force him to see that you have confidence in what you're offering. Far from being required to dispense answers on cue like some kind of trained monkey, **you see your real mission as being to help the prospect reason out the answers for himself.** (If your instinct is to shy away from this approach — to feel, instead, that your prospects will never rise to the challenge — then, again, you are prospecting people you don't like. That's *your* fault, not theirs.)

At the end of the five-second silence, when you know you've got his full attention, you can drop the other shoe:

PROSPECT: *I can do better in bonds.*

SUPERSTAR: *I hope so.*

(5 second pause)

SUPERSTAR: *You see, this all-cash RELP can't possibly start out yielding more than 6% or 7%, when you and I both know you could buy a double-A rated, ten-year corporate bond yielding nearly 9%.*

But every year, with excellent management, rents, cash flows and property values in good real estate can go up.

The bond won't. Ten years from now, the bond will still be giving you the same income. And then it'll pay you back the same paper dollars you bought it with.

I'm recommending that you put just 15% of

your pension assets in real estate. You're welcome to keep the other 85% in bonds, if you'd like.

And I meant what I said: I hope inflation stays so low over the next decade that your bonds outperform my real estate. Frankly, we'd all be better off.

But are you really willing to bet your whole portfolio that inflation's over for good?

See what we mean? After all, give this fellow a break — he doesn't understand real estate. He knows the ten-year AA corporate market yields close to 9%. All you said was that your RELP would start out yielding 6%. Who could blame him for seizing on those two numbers and jumping to the erroneous conclusion that nine is better than six? Nobody. But the fact is that it isn't as simple as that. And, moreover, you're only talking about diversifying a small portion of the plan's assets.

Now, you could have lectured at him with both those points in your presentation. Sure. But isn't it so much stronger, and healthier, to bring those points out in response to his own question, so that at least you can be sure he's still listening? You bet it is. And that's what a non-answer answer sets you up to accomplish.

Answering a question with a question works pretty much the same way:

PROSPECT: *What if I get audited?*

SUPERSTAR: *What if you do?*

(5 second pause)

SUPERSTAR: *After all, you can never lose a partnership deduction as a result of an audit of your individual return.*

If they see something they don't like, they

have to go upstream to the partnership's tax return to see if they can pick that apart.

In fact, this type of RELP has been audited several times and the result is always the same: no lost deductions. The tax assumptions in this RELP are, after all, pretty tame.

Is that what you're talking about, or are you concerned about something else on your tax return?

When you think about it, the question about an audit can only mean one of two things: (1) the prospect still doesn't believe in your RELP, but he doesn't know exactly how to put his fear into words; or (2) there are other aspects of his tax return that will not stand the light of an audit.

Usually it's the former. But, the amateur RELP salesperson blunders into an *overstated* answer: "No, you won't be audited," or, even worse, "This type of RELP has never been audited." (Incidentally, who'd want a RELP that's never been audited? That's like saying: Buy this bullet-proof vest because nobody's ever been fired on while wearing one. It completely misses the point.) The prospect feels that his worse fears are confirmed: He's dealing with a lightweight.

The overriding message is: **Never speak directly to a stated objection — assume, instead, that it is not a clear statement of the client's real concern.** Respond either with another question, or with a non-answer answer. This approach shakes up the prospect's thinking, buys you some time to try to figure out what's really on his mind, and blunts the force of his question.

With most people, the more reasonable you are, the more reasonable they'll be. You just have to give each other time to see that you're both being reasonable.

Wrangling like a high-school debater over every question or objection isn't a very smart way to show you're reasonable. Think of the Kennedy-Nixon debates in 1960. Kennedy spoke always to the television audience, and always to the larger issues that he thought people really cared about. Nixon, following the narrow definition of the format, "debated" each of Kennedy's points, trying to refute them. Those debates probably changed the outcome of the election.

Here are some other ways of responding so that the effect is to startle the prospect slightly, to reinforce the impression that questions don't disturb your confidence, and to force him to rethink his own question.

PROSPECT: *I don't think hotels are a good investment right now.*

SUPERSTAR: *Why?*

Think of the volumes of good things that happen when you say, "Why?" The amateur RELP salesperson will just regurgitate three key facts/statistics from the sales brochure about the nifty economics of hotels, because he takes the question *at face value.* The superstar sees the client's question as a vague, ill-defined reaction to something troubling. But he doesn't know what it is. So, he doesn't answer — he *questions.* He helps the prospect formulate his concerns, in a low-pressure style. And he learns more that way:

PROSPECT: *I read an article in a magazine that said that hotels were overbuilt.*

                        (Now we're getting someplace. Now for the first time we have an objection that may be worth speaking to.)

SUPERSTAR: *I'm sure that, in some places and with some kinds of hotels, that must be true.*
                        In fact, all real estate is like that: It gets overbuilt in some places, and not in others. The office building market in Houston has been

weak, for instance, but at the same time the midtown Manhattan market is strong.

Something, somewhere is always overbuilt. And it's a great opportunity someplace else. That's why you're hiring this RELP sponsor to be your asset manager.

That's what a RELP general partner really is, by the way: an asset manager. And you hire him to find you good opportunities wherever they are. Do you see what I mean?

Now, just suppose this colloquy had gone another way:

PROSPECT: *I don't think hotels are a good investment right now.*

SUPERSTAR: *Why?*

PROSPECT: *Every time I drive by that big new Scotch Plaid Inn downtown, there aren't any cars in the parking lot.*

Do you see what's happening here? If you proceed from the conscious realization that people don't really know that much about real estate, you'll be on the lookout for objections, like these two, which are based on fragmentary, half-formed impressions. And you want to turn them aside as gently as you can, because they aren't real. (In response to the Scotch Plaid Inn objection, the superstar grins, and says, "Guess we'd better not buy *that* one, then." And then he doesn't say anything else. All the truly great salespeople in the world are masters of the art of shutting up.) Start by asking, "Why?"

Or, where it's appropriate:

CONSIDER SAYING
"THAT'S RIGHT."

Here's an example:

PROSPECT: *Buying leveraged real estate is dangerous. You could get foreclosed.*

SUPERSTAR: *That's right.*

(Silence)

The RELP amateur will jump right in and give the prospect seventeen reasons why he won't be foreclosed. And he'll come off looking just like every other securities salesperson who says to his client, in effect: "Buy this investment, because all the good things *will* happen, and all the bad things *won't* happen." And then he wonders why nobody believes him. Isn't that an awful way to go through life?

The superstar sits back and says to himself, "That's right, Jack. There is a doomsday risk in this style of investing, as there is in every other. And you've identified it. Now, what are you going to do with it?" Because he knows that the prospect is (without consciously meaning to do so) trying to draw him into a false position, he is (with the greatest courtesy) refusing to be drawn. Saying, "That's right," and then not saying anything else, forces the prospect to amplify the question, or explain it, or narrow its focus, or *something*. But when he speaks again, he'll have clarified the issue for both of you.

PROSPECT: *Well, don't you think I should be concerned about that?*

SUPERSTAR: *I most certainly do. You see, we've agreed that you need superior capital growth. And we've agreed that leveraged real estate is one proven way of accomplishing this goal.*
             And now we've agreed that, at the extreme, foreclosure — the loss of your investment in a property — is the doomsday risk.

Actually, your decision is pretty simple: You can't have access to those potential rewards without accepting that potential risk. I know that's not an answer, but I think it is a useful way of restating the question.

My real answer, of course, is this RELP. And, even more important, this general partner.

(Optional)

We covered the fact that this RELP will own 8 to 10 properties. Let's suppose we lose one. It's never happened to any of this sponsor's RELPs, but let's suppose it does. You'd lose, for argument's sake, 10% to 12½% of your capital. And even that small wound could be healed, in a year or two, by appreciation in the rest of the portfolio, assuming they just do Ok. Does that seem like an acceptable risk?

(Standard)

You just don't do leveraged real estate investing without a large, well-capitalized and deeply committed real estate partner.

That's why, out of an army of these people who try to do business with us, we chose Brixnstix. You need someone with a clear history of acquiring properties that perform well.

And even more, you need a partner who, when he does make a mistake, will commit the capital and people it takes to turn the thing around. After all, time and money cure all ills in real estate. Can you see that?

Whenever the client states an obvious risk or limitation in any style of real estate, agree with him by saying, "That's right." And then wait for him to put the question or objection in a clearer context. Because, remember, less than five minutes ago, in your conceptual presentation, he agreed that this type of real estate investing could be good for him.

Here's another example:

PROSPECT: *There's no assurance that this RELP can continue to produce the kinds of returns shown on this track-record page.*

SUPERSTAR: *That's right.*

(Silence)

Alternatively, you may hear this objection in a couple of different ways:

PROSPECT: *Inflation is very low now. I don't think you can get these kinds of returns any more.*

SUPERSTAR: *You may be right.*

(Silence)

Or

PROSPECT: *How do you know this RELP can keep producing these kinds of returns?*

SUPERSTAR: *I don't.*

(Silence)

What is the prospect trying to do here? Perhaps without realizing it, he's trying to get you to hang your hat on a number (the track record, the projections in a private placement, whatever). For his own sake, you can't let him make the number, rather than the concept, the central issue.

Remember, you're selling exposure, not proof. The particular numbers don't interest you that much. You know that, over *any* intermediate-term period, real estate can outperform other securities the prospect may invest in. Although this client hasn't fully focused on it yet, real estate is *one* suitable investment in a portfolio, not the *only* investment. (In this regard, it's sometimes worth illustrating the portfolio approach. Remind the client that, if he had walked in off the street with $1 million in a shoebox, and asked, "Should I buy stocks, or bonds, or real estate?" you would have correctly answered, "Yes.")

So, in the silence that follows your non-answer answer to the track record issue, what will the prospect say?

PROSPECT: *Well, if you can't be sure of the numbers, why do you recommend that I buy it?*

SUPERSTAR: *First, let me tell you why I'm not interested in the specific numbers.*

Real estate is an operating business, and the number of factors that go into making it a successful business are too great to be measured exactly in advance.

When you and I agreed, a few minutes ago, about real estate's ability to address some of your financial goals, it wasn't based on any particular number. And it shouldn't be.

Instead, we should be able to agree that real estate, being essentially illiquid, has to produce generally superior returns, relative to other investments.

It's that relative superiority, rather than any absolute number, that we should keep focusing on. And the other thing we want to remember is that real estate is just one of several investment opportunities, so that we're properly diversified. Do you see what I mean?

Here again, you have profited from the number of conceptual points of agreement that you'd previously established during your five-minute presentation. The amateur RELP salesperson doesn't see this. In his nervousness about Q&A, he let's any question become the whole focus of the discussion. The superstar, on the other hand, says, in effect: "Wait a minute . . . This is certainly an interesting little question, but it's only part of a much larger conceptual framework, most of which, Mr. Prospect, *you've already agreed to.*"

You have to develop a sense of the relative weight of questions to do this really well. In other words, your ability to turn a question around gently on the prospect will be enhanced by an appreciation of how important — or how peripheral — each particular question really is. This experience is just one more reason (if you still needed another one) that *only* the act of practicing your presentation skills, as opposed to the act of learning more facts, leads to RELP superstardom. They don't pay Pavarotti for how well he reads music; they pay him for how he makes the music sound when he sings.

You also have to temper your competitive sales instincts — the visceral urge to drop-kick the objection through the goal post of life — with a little human warmth and understanding. Look . . . this prospect knows he's coming closer and closer to having to make a decision. And he'd rather not do that. This is not, after all, 100 shares of stock. When he buys it, he's committed to it. He knows that, and he unconsciously rebels against the conflict involved in having to make the decision. So he's liable to say anything by way of an objection, or try to hang the conversation up on any small debating point. That's why you never speak directly to the stated objection — because you're pretty sure it doesn't have much to do with what's really troubling your prospect.

Have a little sympathy for him. Smile. See if you can **learn**

to stay mentally tough, but in a soothing kind of way. And remind him that this is, after all, a cooperative process. You're both working through a shared perception of his investment goals, and you've both agreed on a particular form of real estate investing which fulfills those goals. If you hadn't, the conversation never would have gotten this far.

You'll notice that all the hypothetical answers in this chapter accomplish the same thing. They:

TAKE THE PROSPECT BACK
TO THE LAST ESTABLISHED LEVEL
OF COMMON UNDERSTANDING.

When you say, "We've agreed that . . . ," what you're doing is steadfastly refusing to allow the Q&A process to draw the focus of the conversation away from the larger, agreed-upon principles. Because you know that, if you let that happen, the sales interview will degenerate into an endless ping pong game, played without a ball.

ADDING BACKSPIN

In addition to the two basic techniques (answering a question with a question or offering a provocative non-answer answer), there's another effective way to (quite literally) turn the prospect's question around. And that is simply to repeat it, either with or without the preface, "I'm not sure I understand your question."

EXAMPLE

PROSPECT: *If these are such great real estate operators, what do they need me for?*

SUPERSTAR: *I'm not sure I understand your question. Are you asking why a real estate operator needs equity partners?*

When you get good at this, you'll be able to turn the question around with some backspin so it's already half-answered by the way you rephrase it.

As in all of the techniques recommended in this chapter, be careful to express your responses in a sincere and genuinely thought-provoking way. Avoid being smart-alecky, like this:

PROSPECT: *If these are such great real estate operators, what do they need me for?*

SALESPERSON: *If IBM is such a great company, why do they have to sell stock to the public?*

See what we mean? This answer (or rather, this answering a question with a question) is not wrong. In fact, it correctly suggests that all great capital-intensive businesses can most effectively leverage off other people's capital. But that idea comes out, in this example, with an argumentative under-tone. That kind of adversarial flavoring will usually poison a sales interview. In fact, **all the great salespeople know that arguments in a sales context are unwinnable,** much like arguments about religion or politics.

Being argumentative is a fairly easy trap to fall into. You've been working hard to learn all you can about a RELP. You've actually invested in it yourself, and you're just sure it's right for the prospect you're talking to. If you find him asking "smoking gun" questions (which seem to communicate a feeling that there's got to be something fundamentally wrong with your RELP), you can find yourself getting angry. And you'll be tempted to respond in kind.

Don't do it! Just sit back and think. Maybe people distrust your prospect all day long and make him prove everything he says. Or maybe he's just made this way. Maybe he just feels that, to get his capital, you're really going to have to work for it. Relax. It's business; it's not personal. Don't let anybody take you off the track. **Don't let anybody set your**

agenda. Mode Q&A is the hardest time to keep that in mind. But it's also the most critical time.

WASH AWAY THE LIQUIDITY OBJECTION

Restating the question is also the single most effective way of shaping your answer to the liquidity argument.

PROSPECT: *I don't want to be tied up in this thing for seven years.*

SUPERSTAR: *I'm not sure I understand your question. Are you saying there's a good chance you'll need this money for something else during that time?*

PROSPECT: *Well, no, when you put it that way . . . I guess it just makes me uncomfortable.*

SUPERSTAR: *(With a big smile): Welcome to the club. The exact same thing happened to me the first time I invested in a RELP.*

You get into a mental bind that says: Gee, I don't completely understand this thing. And if I buy it, I'm pretty well locked into it for some number of years.

And you freeze. We all do. But then you realize that you can't have the unique benefits of real estate without accepting the illiquidity .

And when you understand that trade off, your concern about liquidity just kind of fades away.

Don't you feel that's true?

This style of objection handling continues the practice in which the salesperson draws attention constantly to the financial and psychological situations that he and the client share. Making common cause with the clients in your "natural market" should be relatively easy, once you start consciously practicing it. We've already established that you and your clients have a great deal in common.

The poor amateur who constantly tries to overcome objections with fact and reason misses more than a lot of sales. He misses the opportunity to let his prospect *ventilate* his feelings. And thus he misses the chance to *validate* those feelings by demonstrating that he, and lots of other people, feel the same way.

Making a real emotional connection with the client leads to the best selling. One sure way to insure that you're never in any danger of connecting is to answer the stated objection. That's because the prospect's stated objection never means what he feels.

Listen to what the RELP superstar sounds like:

SUPERSTAR RESPONSES

Why?
What do you mean?
I'm not sure I understand. Are you asking . . .
That's a very valid concern.
Why does that bother you?
We all feel like that.
Do you see what I mean?
That's interesting; I'd never looked at it that way.
Don't you feel that's true?
Don't you agree . . .

All of those responses say: I'm open; I'm interested; I care about the way you feel; I'm thinking about what you said; I want to understand you . . . and (last but certainly not least) I'm confident that we will reach agreement. It's very hard (though not impossible) for a prospect to stay rigid, cold and challenging when you deal with him in this way. When he does continue to be stiff and adversarial, what he's really telling you is that he doesn't care what you say. He's made up his mind that he isn't going to do business with you. And, he's probably never going to tell you why.

"C'est la vie," thinks the superstar. "You're just another hashmark on my daily baseline prospecting calendar. I just have to let you disqualify yourself, if that's what you've made up your mind to do."

CONQUER THE MOUNT EVEREST OF OBJECTIONS

Now, please try to maintain that sense of perfect calm and serenity as we set out to climb the Mount Everest of RELP objections: "THE FEES ARE TOO HIGH."

Actually, this is a good place to pause for a moment, and ask you to take a spot quiz, just to see whether you're getting the *real* Q&A message. Here goes:

SPOT QUIZ

The correct answer to the objection, "The fees are too high," is:

A. *That's a very handsome tie you're wearing.*
B. *No, they're not.*
C. *I have to let you disqualify yourself, if that's what you've made up your mind to do.*
D. *In relation to what?*
E. *Actually, it has a Stanger "deal terms" rating of AA (79.7), which is higher than any similar RELP.*
F. *Have a nice day.*

Let's do this by process of elimination. First of all, it isn't A, and it isn't F. Those are non-answer answers, all right, but not in the thought-provoking way we recommend this particular technique. It isn't C, either, at least not yet. Don't be a quitter.

You know it can't be B, because that's argumentative. And E is definitely out, because it commits two cardinal sins. First, E speaks directly to the stated objection. Second, it's pure jargon. (And why would you assume he means "too high in relation to other RELPs?")

Which leaves you with D. Relaxed, gently challenging, answering-a-question-with-a-question D:

"IN RELATION TO WHAT?"

What does the prospect mean? What is he comparing the RELP to? Is he talking about buying his own property? The answer to these and many other questions is the same: The salesperson has no idea yet. Since he doesn't understand the question, he won't say anything; he'll ask, "In relation to what?"

This client is driving around in a Mercedes. If he ever found out what it cost when it rolled off the assembly line in Stuttgart versus what he paid for it in the dealer's showroom in Phoenix, Arizona, all his hair would turn white and then fall out. He's wearing a suit that he bought from the fanciest haberdasher in town for $325. If he ever finds out it cost $29.68 to make in Singapore, he'll have apoplexy. Now, is this person really worried about *"markup?"* Not when you put it to him that way.

"Markup" is a phony issue, anyway. First of all, a public RELP prospectus is one of the only places you're ever going to find what the "markup" actually is. That's something to be grateful for, not critical of.

But even beyond that, listen to the logic of what this prospect is saying. First, you told him your firm chose this

RELP sponsor above a whole host of others you could have picked, and you told him three distinguishing features of the sponsor's superior capabilities. Next (if it's true), you told him that you've personally invested with these people. And, now, within five minutes, he's turned around and said that he's found an objectively fatal flaw in the deal. At the very least, he has implicitly said that you and your firm don't know what you're doing in real estate . . . *and he does.* That doesn't really make any sense, so there must be something even deeper and more sinister at work here.

And there is. The prospect walked hand in hand with you through your whole conceptual presentation (who these people are, how you chose them, how comfortable you are with them). If he still says, when asked for an investment decision, "The fees are too high," what he really means is:

"I DON'T BELIEVE/TRUST YOU YET."

There is no other possible answer that works, because there is no logic to this pattern of events. The prospect has probably never looked at an investment in which all the costs are so clearly defined, and he just doesn't know what to relate them to.

So start slowly. Remember that the serious prospect probably wants to be reassured. Probe around for a way to calm him down, and to re-establish the natural connection you had during the conceptual presentation, when he was easily agreeing with you. Listen, first, to his answer to the question, "In relation to what?"

You see, he didn't expect you to say anything even remotely like that. And he certainly has no ready answer to the question. So whatever he says will, for better or worse, be very revealing. Fairly often, the surprise of your question will prompt a reasonably open response: "I don't know," or "It just seems terribly expensive," or something equally unfocused.

When you find the conversation returning, in that way, to some kind of real dialogue, there are a couple of tacks you can take.

One is to **steer the discussion back to the superiority of the RELP sponsor.** Businesspeople, in particular, will respond to the idea that you can hire the very best people in an industry, or you can hire people to work inexpensively. But you can never, ever hire the best people in an industry — people who've worked for years to build a reputation, a credible record, and real net worth — to work inexpensively. This approach tends to blunt the force of the argument very effectively.

Another approach is to **remind the prospect, gently but firmly, that the RELP industry is now a very mature and closely researched business, functioning in a price-competitive way.** The fact that a prospect may never have examined the pricing structure of RELPs before is perfectly understandable, but not particularly relevant: Your firm is monitoring fees constantly and in minute detail. There are easily comprehensible, apples-to-apples ways of doing price comparisons on public RELPs. So you ought to be able to quietly and confidently put the idea that a particular RELP is wildly overpriced — absolutely, or relative to its good competitors — to rest.

If you're showing a leveraged equity RELP to a prospect, you have to consider the fees as a percentage of total purchase price — debt and equity. You'll want to stress (but *never* as a direct response to the objection) that you can't look at fees just as a percentage of the investors' capital contributions. Syndicators have been trying to point out since the dawn of recorded time (well, since 1974, anyway) that buying a RELP may turn out to be less expensive, in terms of commissions and fees, than buying your house.

Suppose you bought a $150,000 house with 25% down and a mortgage for the rest. Your friendly real estate broker gets 6% of the purchase price as a commission, so that's

$9,000. Figure you'll pay the bank a 2% commitment fee ("points") for your $112,500 mortgage: another $2,250. Maybe if your brother-in-law is a lawyer (heaven help you), you'll be able to hold other closing costs to $1,000. That's a total of $12,250 in "fees" — a whopping 33% "markup" on your $37,500 down payment. Compare that with any reputable RELP. If you're prospect doesn't swallow real hard . . . you haven't got a prospect. (The buying-a-home analogy is a whiskery old comparison. But remember: Things get to be clichés by always being true.)

In asking your prospect what he's relating the fees in a RELP to, you may, even in this day and age, hear this one: "I can buy rental property more cheaply on my own."

With inflation in property values, you tend to hear this less and less. Back in the '70s, when you could buy a fourplex in Pismo Beach for $100,000 ($15,000 down, and a mortgage), it was a more common objection. It wasn't any more true then than it is now, of course. You still paid a real estate commission, points, and closing costs. And your sophisticated, price-conscious prospect got to enjoy the thrill of being the midnight-toilet-fixer-of-last-resort for whichever Hell's Angel happened to be using his property as a crash pad that week. (Yes, *week*. Tenants you have in a place like that always skip out before the first of the month . . . You mean the real estate broker didn't tell you that?)

The I-can do it-myself issue isn't big anymore. A little apartment building with sixty 800-square foot apartments can go for $1.5 million these days. And the expense and management-intensiveness of owning and renting an individual condo will age you very quickly. If your prospect really thinks he can select, negotiate, acquire, manage and sell *anything* more efficiently than a real estate operator with $1 billion in property and a staff of 500 . . . well, let him. You're a communicator/salesperson, not a psychotherapist. There's just so much you can do for people.

Costs in a first-quality public RELP are just not a major debating point (although they may be in private placements). Moreover, a prospect is usually raising the issue as a smoke screen for something else that's bothering him — something that's harder for him to understand and articulate. Stop listening to what he's saying. Find out what he *means*.

SUMMARY

- How you answer objections is more valuable to learn than what to say.

- There is no smoking gun.

- The stated question or objection is not the real question or objection.

- The non-answer answer, answering a question with a question and repeating the question are techniques giving you back control and initiative.

- Always return to the established common ground in your answer.

- Give empathy, not hard answers.

- The high fee objection is a high, soft lob to your forehand when you're at the net . . . the easiest shot to put away.

14

Questions & Answers II: The Most Powerful Response and the Close

We come now to the greatest, most wonderful, most liberating, most useful response imaginable. It's perfectly applicable to an almost infinite number of investor questions. And, as promised in Chapter 2, you will get to use this response at least once in every RELP sales interview for the next two years. It is, of course,

"I DON'T KNOW."

This answer is something you really want to spend a lot of time on, because its psychological and practical uses are so powerful. "I don't know" is the *ultimate* non-answer answer, which, when used properly, completely changes the direction of your conversation. You will regain control of the sales interview, which you had originally during your presentation but gave up, little by little, as you moved deeper into Mode Q&A.

The RELP superstar knows that "I don't know" is his best friend. The amateur fears it pathologically. The superstar *can't wait* to be asked a question to which he doesn't know the answer. In fact, in order to hasten the interview to a successful conclusion, the superstar may say, "I don't know," even when he's got a pretty fair idea of what the answer is, or at least where he might find it. The amateur not only doesn't use this tactic, he can't even believe it exists.

The superstar knows that, when he says "I don't know," he regains all the initiative. When the amateur is finally forced to say, "I don't know," he feels that he should have known, and that he has failed. And yet they're both reacting to the very same question.

How is this possible? How can one salesperson, asked a question he can't answer, close the transaction in the next five minutes, while another salesperson, asked the same question, lets his inability to answer zero out his ego and allow the sales interview to wind down into failure?

Well, it certainly can't be product knowledge, can it? We've already agreed that neither of them knows the answer. So, first and foremost, it must have something to do with *attitude*.

Even as he struggles up the learning curve, the emerging RELP superstar is convinced that he is in possession of the most important conceptual truths about a RELP and its managers. He has stipulated to the Q&A Warranty: that for twenty-four months, or 240 sales interviews, whichever comes later, he's going to be asked a question he can't answer. So he has prepared a fall-back position which works *every time*.

The emerging RELP washout has never been able to shake the psychology which says: "I'm supposed to know this stuff." He has not accepted the inevitability of a question he can't answer. So he has no fall-back. He has only fear. And fear kills confidence. So this poor fellow is already on a downward spiral, which inevitably ends, as he feared it would, in failure.

(The other thing the washout never accepted was that RELP prospecting is a numbers game. He has his ego invested in the outcome of every single RELP presentation, so that each inevitable failure is a real blow to his self-confidence.

He takes it as a rejection of him. And then he wonders why he can't complete his RELP prospecting program.)

In what way is the attitude of the emerging RELP superstar different? And what is the fall-back position which he's put in place in order to make the question he can't answer the jumping-off point for closing the sale? Well, first and foremost:

THE SUPERSTAR IS NOT AFRAID.

We keep saying this again and again, but that's just how important it is. During Mode Q&A, the prospect is probing, not just for how much the salesperson knows, but for a sense of how genuinely *confident* he is in his RELP. The lighter, easier, and more succinct the salesperson is, the more the prospect receives the subliminal message: "I have perfect confidence in this RELP's superiority and in the fact that it's a marvelous fit for you, my client."

When you get to the moment of truth, and you are asked a question you can't answer, the fact that you are not disconcerted has a tremendous impact on the prospect. The ability to sit there, smile, shrug, and say, "I don't know" — *and then not say anything else for a few moments* — tells the prospect in the most forceful way that your unshakable conviction isn't based on an endless accumulation of small details but on the higher realities of the RELP and its people.

This attitude says (nonverbally), "Stop! You're looking for the truth in the wrong places. I don't know the answer to that question, and it should be clear to you that the fact that I don't know doesn't concern me — or even particularly interest me."

And in those few moments of silence, the prospect looks at you, sitting there in an attitude of perfect calm . . . and suddenly hears what you have *really* said:

VERBAL: *I don't know.*

NONVERBAL: *And, therefore, it's probably not important.*

That's the beginning of why the superstar welcomes the question he can't answer. Since he is selling himself (as opposed to selling the number of technical details he knows), the superstar wants to steer the focus of the conversation back to himself, and to the paramount issue of the RELP.

And that points up yet another reason why it's so important to own a little bit of the RELP you love to sell. Because when you do own it, and you've made your prospect aware of that fact during your conceptual presentation, then the nonverbal "other shoe" drops with an even louder thud:

VERBAL: *I don't know.*

NONVERBAL: *And I'm an investment professional who bought this for his own account. So if I didn't care enough to investigate this particular point, it must not matter.*

The "I don't know" response has the added benefit (particularly if the interview has been in Mode Q&A for a while) of drawing the presentation to an end. The silent suggestion is that you've been through all the major deal points, and the questions are now getting irrelevant.

But, other than through instinct, what makes the emerging superstar so sure that this question isn't material to the investment decision? That's easy:

THE SUPERSTAR KNOWS
WHAT ALL THE IMPORTANT QUESTIONS ARE.

Wouldn't you? After all, if you're committed to present this RELP at least once (and perhaps more times) *every day,* you wouldn't do so without first sitting down with the wholesaler, or your firm's sales professionals, and asking:

"What are the ten most common/most important questions or objections about this RELP?"

Don't accept fast answers to this question, either. Make everybody take time and really work out the big questions/objections, and the answers. If there's more than one person you can ask, by the way, ask them separately, without explaining that you've done so. Then compare and contrast their lists, looking very hard at the differences, and probing for why they're different.

That way, when you're in a sales interview, you'll know your presentation cold and know the answers to the major inquiries you're going to be running into. When Mode Q&A wanders beyond your list, you'll have a pretty strong feeling that the conversation is drifting, and you can start to close it off with your serene and imperturbable "I don't know."

(The RELP washout never learns this technique. He unconsciously accepts the validity of any and every question just because the client asked it. That's very sad.)

Now, suppose you say, "I don't know," and you just sit there, calmly saying nothing . . . but the prospect doesn't say anything either. This is a somewhat different kettle of fish. Now you're in a situation where you'd better go ahead and gently ask:

"Is that important to you?"

The answer may very well be, "I don't suppose it matters much," which is, in every case, a signal to begin your close. Because the prospect has, without realizing it, acknowledged that he's about out of important questions.

But suppose the prospect says, "Yes, I think I'd really need to know the answer to that." Or suppose he didn't even wait for you to ask, "Is that important to you?" What if, as soon as you said, "I don't know," he said "Well, I'd really have to know that in order to make a decision?" He thinks the interview is over, right? (If he were talking to an emerging RELP washout, he'd be all too correct.)

Wrong. Because now comes the ultimate fall-back position:

THE SUPERSTAR GOES TO HIS BACKUP MAN.

THE BACKUP MAN: DON'T LEAVE HOME WITHOUT ONE

This technique is so elegant, so simple and so genuinely inevitable that it takes an intensely creative emerging RELP washout *not* to think of it. Observe closely, please.

You've long since accepted our solemn assurance that, for at least two years after reading this book, you'll be asked a question you can't answer in every sales interview you have.

Now, it's wonderful that you've formulated and mastered your list of the ten most important questions/objections, so that you are totally conversant with the genuine make-or-break issues in your RELP. There's just one little problem: Either the prospect hasn't got a list, or the prospect's list is different from yours.

And so there will inevitably come that moment when you don't know an answer to a question that the prospect thinks (or claims to think — which is, for all practical purposes, the same thing) is important. What can you do? Just one thing.

You look your prospect right in the eye, and say:

"I'm sure we can get the answer to that question by making a simple phone call. May I do that?"

There isn't any way the prospect can say "No" without signaling that he doesn't really care what the answer is. He has to let you make the call, or disqualify himself because he's made up his mind not to do business with you.

Who are you going to call? Your backup person, of course. Because under no circumstances should you, at any time during your two-year superstar apprenticeship, ever go out on an appointment, or make an appointment to have someone come into your office for a presentation, unless you

HAVE SOMEONE FROM THE RELP, OR FROM YOUR OWN FIRM, IN HIS OFFICE WAITING TO TAKE YOUR CALL.

Never make an appointment for a RELP sales interview without reaching an agreement with a specific person that he'll be near his phone when you're out there trying to do business for him. That's all there is to it.

After all, **there is nothing quite as effective as the third-party, call-on-the-expert close.** And when you know you have someone backing you up, you no longer have to be concerned in the least about being asked a question you can't answer. You know you have instant access to a friendly, knowledgeable voice who, as your client can clearly hear, knows who you are and welcomes your call. Given the backup person, why would you ever again worry about questions you can't answer? (The willingness and ability of a RELP to provide you with nice, knowledgeable backup people is an acid test of whether you should work to raise money for them. If they can't be bothered with backing you up, you can't be bothered selling their RELP. Over and out.)

Of course, when you invite your prospect to restate his question to your backup person, you'll find that half the force of the question has already dissipated. That's simply because the prospect recognized the fact that you really are a super professional, and that this RELP and its people really are quite well known to you. Remember that the question itself may not have been a true expression of what's really bothering the prospect; there may still have been some lingering doubt in his mind about the relationship among you, your firm, and this RELP sponsor. Your ability effortlessly to go to the backup person can't help but alleviate those concerns.

If credibility were all this technique accomplished, it would be worth using. But that isn't all it accomplishes. **Going to the backup person moves the sales interview from Mode Q&A to a close.** A little gentle prodding from you is needed to make the transition, but that's easily done.

When your client has restated the question you couldn't (or wouldn't) answer, your backup person will, of course, have a very logical and compelling answer. (Remember: There is no smoking gun.) At that point, you come back into the conversation, by asking this question:

> *"Before we let (backup person) off the phone, are there any other questions or problems on your mind that would prevent you from making this investment today?"*

Think about it. Wouldn't you have felt awfully dumb if you'd called the backup person, gotten the answer, hung up, and then had the prospect ask you another question you couldn't answer? Sure. So the idea is to keep everyone on the phone until all questions are smoked out and answered. Now the prospect is in a position to make an intelligent decision, *right then and there.*

This technique is also an effective way of short-circuiting some of the more obvious stalling to which a prospect may resort. Picture a situation where someone is sitting in your office, and you've got him on a conference phone with an executive of a major real estate sponsor. After all that, will the prospect say he has to talk it over with his wife? Not likely.

The backup person is probably the single most effective tool you can use to get you past the constant anxiety of the infinite number of technical questions to which you don't know the answer. And you can't grow into a truly effective RELP communicator/salesperson if you live under that cloud. The day will surely come when that anxiety is gone. You will have progressively learned more and more of the elusive answers, so that your need for the backup person withers away. But until that day comes: no backup person, no appointment.

THE ULTIMATE DISQUALIFIER

Speaking of stalls, by the way, there are few that are quite as ludicrous in public RELP sales as when the prospect says he has to show a prospectus to his accountant or attorney. (In private placements, by contrast, the CPA may be the critical player in the decision-making process.) This is about as close as you come to the ultimate prospect disqualifier. In fact, let us postulate a rule on the subject:

UNLESS THE PROPOSED INVESTMENT IS OVER $20,000 OR UNLESS THE SALE IS TO A PENSION PLAN, THE PROSPECT WHO SAYS HE'S GOING TO CONSULT HIS CPA IS, IN FACT, NO PROSPECT.

You can probe around for a while, if you have the energy, but we doubt that much will come of it. Start the way you would when you hear any off-the-wall comment (one which, in other words, is so far off the beaten track that you don't have a relaxed, practical answer to it). Ask "Why?" (Again: There's no rule that says the prospect gets to ask all the questions.) Usually, the prospect will say something to the effect that he wants the CPA to tell him if it's a good deal or not.

Isn't that depressing? Here you've spent all this time establishing a need, talking about how well your firm knows these people, and what makes them superior operators, telling the prospect (if it's true) that you own the RELP yourself . . . and he says he wants his CPA to tell him if it's good. What is he really telling you? "You've told me it's good, but I don't believe you." Let him go. He's not going to show it to his CPA, of course, and who cares? You're never going to do any significant business with this person because he doesn't trust you. There's no communication. This prospect has bond/CD buyer written all over him: He only believes, heaven help us, in "guarantees."

The only kind of salesperson who is upset by someone like this is one who isn't making enough calls. No emerging superstar gives this kind of prospect a second thought. In the time it takes you to sit there wondering what you could have possibly said to this bird, you can make two more calls. Move on: He was just another hash mark on your "baseline" call chart.

MOVING PAST A COMMON STALL

That's not to say that there aren't a number of very effective stalls. There are. The most common among them is: "I'd like to think it over."

When you hear that one, all you have to say is:

> "You absolutely do. Nobody should ever be encouraged to jump into an essentially illiquid investment like real estate. On the other hand, nobody should be in the position — which you and I have both been in, I'll bet — of letting a good real estate opportunity slip by, and then biting our tongues when we see what it's worth a year later. When you do think this over, will you be focusing primarily on the integrity of the people?"

And now you're going to go down a laundry list of all the fine things about the RELP that he already agreed were attractive. "Are you going to think about the fairness of the business deal? Are you going to think about the wisdom of being a mortgage lender instead of a property owner?"

The prospect's inclination will be to keep saying no, that each of those aspects of the deal is actually quite good. And you'll have gotten to do a very quick summation of the best features of your RELP.

When no concrete objection surfaces, you'll want to say:

"It's really just the difficulty of making the decision, isn't it? (Don't wait for the answer.) *I understand that; I struggle with it all the time myself. Let me just ask you one thing: HOW WOULD YOU FEEL TODAY IF YOU'D PASSED UP THE CHANCE TO BUY YOUR HOUSE?"*

That's really the ultimate cruncher. And it's one of the most powerful ideas the RELP salesperson has going for him: The persistent feeling that, over time, real estate investments do well for people, and that, more often than not, when people have procrastinated and let real estate investment opportunities slip by, they've regretted it later on. So be ready for a delaying question, play it back through a list of things that reinforce your RELP's attractiveness, and end with the question of how the prospect would feel about having missed out on his home. See if that doesn't speed up his decision-making process.

ISOLATE THE BLOCK

Our theory about closing is generally consistent with everything else you've read in this chapter: The reason that a prospect gives you for not investing in your RELP is not the reason he's not investing in your RELP. So the challenge is to get him back to a point where he's comfortable telling you what's really bothering him. Only in that way can you break up his real source of resistance.

The technique is called "isolating the blocking objection." This is a three part system:

(1) Soften the objection by reacting with sympathy and respect.

(2) Ask if this is the single remaining objection that's preventing your prospect from making the investment. In other words, if you could succeed in causing this objection not to be a problem, would the prospect buy the RELP?

(3) Only after hearing an affirmative answer to the previous question, proceed to try to do away with the objection. Then close again.

Here's an example:

SUPERSTAR: *If you haven't any more questions, can I suggest a $20,000 investment to start with now?*

PROSPECT: *I don't think so. I think that the new tax law is going to take away a lot of the incentive to buy real estate, and property prices will actually decline.*

SUPERSTAR: *That's a very reasonable concern. All investment tends to be postponed in an atmosphere of uncertainty. And tax law changes, in particular, tend to make all of us nervous.*
But tell me: If there were some way to relieve that concern — if I could make you reasonably comfortable even with the tax uncertainty — would you have any other concerns that would cause you not to want to own this RELP?

PROSPECT: *No, that's my real problem. There's been too much tax-driven real estate buying. With tax benefits going away, prices will fall.*

SUPERSTAR: Fine. I think the problem may be that you're focused very clearly on the "demand" side of the real estate equation, and what we need to do is look at the "supply" side.

First of all, the people who get hit hardest by tax changes in real estate aren't passive investors like you and me, but the developers of real estate — people who risk their capital to build new property. Tax benefits in real estate were really there to soften that development risk. Take away some of those tax benefits, and you reduce development activity. When new supply decreases but population growth doesn't, eventually you'll get higher rents, and higher — not lower — prices.

And, to tell you the truth, our firm is convinced that even if prices declined a little in the short run — but rents and cash flows didn't — you'd see the huge, non-tax-sensitive buyers, like pension funds, come into the market, snap up the bargains, and drive the market right back up again.

The great thing about real estate is that its value is determined by rents, not by tax laws or market fads. And, in the long run, rents always seem to work higher. Hasn't that always been your experience?

PROSPECT: You can say that again. When I think what my wife and I paid to rent our first apartment in 1960, and what we pay now for our daughter's apartment at college, it's enough to make you cringe.

SUPERSTAR: Exactly. Let's leave short-term swings in the market to the experts, and invest now for the long pull.

PROSPECT: *Sure, when you put it that way . . .*

The foregoing is a nice, simplified example of a case where the stated objection actually did turn out to be the real objection. But look how long and painstaking the superstar's answer was. Now suppose the stated objection was not the real one; look how long you'd have labored, for no productive purpose. Isolating the blocking objection helps insulate you from that risk.

Suppose the conversation had gone this way:

SUPERSTAR: *If you haven't any more questions, can I suggest a $20,000 investment to start with now?*

PROSPECT: *I don't think so. I think that the new tax law is going to take away a lot of the incentive to buy real estate, and property prices will actually decline.*

SUPERSTAR: *That's a very reasonable concern. All investments tend to be posponed in an atmosphere of uncertainty. And tax law changes, in particular, tend to make us all nervous.*
  But, tell me: If there were some way to relieve that concern — if I could make you reasonably comfortable even with the tax uncertainty, would you have any other concerns that would cause you not to want to own this RELP?

PROSPECT: *Well, to tell you the truth, starting three years from now, we'll go through a period where both our daughters are in college for two years. And I'd be afraid we were going to have to use some of that money.*

SUPERSTAR: *Then perhaps we should start with $10,000, and put the rest in a three-year municipal bond.*

PROSPECT: *I'd really sleep a lot better that way.*

Can you see what would have happened if you'd launched into that closely reasoned, macroeconomic analysis of property values, when all the poor fellow cared about was having enough cash for his kid's college? But the only way to avoid that is to isolate the blocking objection — to get the prospect to agree first on what his last remaining problem is.

SUMMARY

- The "I don't know" response is powerful. Say it unafraid and then pause.

- "I don't know" smokes out the prospect and promotes the start of the close.

- "I don't know" moves you into the best closing technique for your RELP sale — using the backup person. Never leave home without one.

- Unless the proposed investment is over $20,000, or is aimed at a pension plan, the CPA stall is a disqualifier.

- Overcome the "I want to think about it" stall with an allusion to how the prospect would feel if he'd missed buying his own home.

- Isolate the blocking objection. Speak to an objection only after the prospect says it's his last one.

15

How to Sell Private Placements: Disqualifying the Prospect

As the emerging superstar becomes more and more conversant with real estate finance and taxation, as well as with increasingly sophisticated ways of prospecting for the big ticket, he eventually wants to tackle the private placement market. And that's one *very* smart decision.

No single strategy can so dramatically affect your business, your income and your net worth as systematically prospecting for private placement clients. These people will make the greatest impact on your career, and nothing forces you to stay focused on them the way private placement prospecting does.

No one who has been in our industry for any length of time can possibly doubt that:

**THE INCOME OF A FINANCIAL
COMMUNICATOR/SALESPERSON
IS AN ABSOLUTE FUNCTION
OF THE INCOMES OF HIS CLIENTS.**

So if you determine to make a significant change in your income and net worth, you ultimately have to raise the median income (and net worth) of your account book.

Everybody can identify high net worth individuals, and everybody is already prospecting them — with stocks, bonds, annuities, life insurance, mutual funds, financial planning and everything else you can think of.

Yet what does this clientele really love to hear about, and talk about? And what is the greatest referral business the financial services industry ever invented? Sure: real estate private placements. That's right. Rumors of the death of private placements, as Mark Twain said of his own widely reported demise, have been greatly exaggerated.

You can start to build a correct and productive view of private placements after tax "reform" by asking yourself, in effect: "Where have all the losses gone?" The answer is, literally, nowhere. The losses are "suspended," that is, trapped inside the deal. (Technically, real estate losses can also still shelter taxable income from other limited partnerships.) They're still there, and can be used to shelter the income produced by the transaction itself, and/or its sale proceeds at the end of the day.

That's wonderful. Because what it tells us is that transactions which can produce high levels of cash income (and therefore a high residual value at the go-out) may now do so largely free of current income taxation for many years. And, lower tax rates significantly augment the after-tax return of deals which are *genuine business winners,* rather than generators of artifical losses. What could be more attractive?

We predict that, in this context, private placements will enjoy a new and wider audience. Because now, staged payments can be planned to coincide with developing levels of cash flow in start-up, turnaround, or new-management situations.

Building a flow of tax-free income and owning great real estate are two of the favorite topics of the high net worth individual. And when you prospect with private RELPs, you immediately distinguish yourself from the crowd of people who are forever yapping at their heels for business. High net worth investors feel they have to (or just want to) listen to private RELP ideas in a way they don't feel they have to listen to all that other stuff.

This news is the best imaginable for the emerging RELP superstar, because:

PRIVATE PLACEMENTS ARE
THE MAJOR LEAGUES.

THE THREE IRRATIONAL FEARS

Still, a complex pattern of reluctance prevents even successful public-RELP salespeople from making a sustained effort in the private area. Examining some of the sources of that hesitancy may be useful, because until you remove the problems, you may not be able to stay with the systematic prospecting program we're about to offer you.

The first is an irrational fear of "big accounts." Remember what we said in Chapter 8 about the importance you attach to the function you perform in relation to the emotional weight you give in your own mind to the prospect's wealth and position.

The RELP washout says, "An important person like Mr. Millions would never want to do business with me. I'm all right dealing with people with household incomes of $50,000 to $75,000, but a guy like that is out of my league." He's right, of course. Someone with his self-image wouldn't last thirty seconds in the prospect's office before he talked himself right back out the door.

The RELP superstar says, "I've been practicing my skills, increasing my knowledge and enjoying growing success in RELPs for a year or two. I've made some pretty nice-sized sales along the way. And I've learned just how many misconceptions people have about real estate finance and taxes. I'll bet I could make a lot of friends, and do a lot of business, if I direct my baseline prospecting program toward private placement buyers. I really believe that my services could be very useful to people with even bigger income and net worth. I think I'll work on *them* for a year, and see what happens."

(The issue of how you see yourself is far beyond the scope of this book. But self-image will turn out to be critical if you're going to try to get a black belt in private placements.)

A second irrational fear is that private placements are very complex, compared to public RELPs (or to anything else, for that matter). Quite the opposite is true. A private placement, almost painfully focused and specific, usually invests in just one important property. There *are* infinitely more detailed numbers and projections than in a public RELP prospectus — that much is true. But, again, all the numbers are built around the operations and financing of one property. When you are working with a capable and experienced private RELP sponsor, they will boil down all the numbers into three to five critical tax and economic issues for you inside of twenty minutes. Your ability to leverage off the sponsor's knowledge of the key variables will just blow the illusion of complexity away.

And the third irrational fear of private placements is our old friend, the fear of being asked a question you can't answer. Looking ignorant in the eyes of your big prospect and his CPA is intimidating. But, as you must realize, private placements are the ultimate arena for the backup person. Forget the two-year, 240-call warranty — in the private area, with the CPA in the picture every time, you're *always* going to be asked questions you can't answer. No backup person, no appointment. Over and out.

So, the three big fears that keep people from making a dent in the private placement market are either inside your own head or totally fictional, depending on how you want to look at them. Still not convinced? That's all right. Here is a list of some of the major attitudes (skills) you've already picked up throughout this book. Far from being specific just to public

RELPs, they're perfectly suited to a complete private placement sales capability, with just a slightly different spin on the ball.

MAJOR ATTITUDES (SKILLS) YOU'VE ACQUIRED

- Selling yourself/selling the GP.
- THE CONCEPT.
- Exposure, not proof (also known as "these are the actual numbers . . . unless they're higher or lower").
- Setting your own agenda.
- Selling what it does, not what it is.
- Selling what you love.
- Stripping away the taxes to get at the real estate economics.
- Time and money cure all ills in real estate.
- The "baseline" prospecting program.
- Leveraging off the wholesaler.
- The issue of tone: The way you say what you say.
- Simplicity: The five-point-presentation.
- Transcending the facts.
- "I'm coming to that."
- Stressing the risks, and how they're managed.
- Empathy: Ventilate and validate.
- Q&A: Non-answer answers, answering a question with a question, and "I don't know."
- The backup man.
- Isolating the blocking objection.

Get the picture? **You already have about 90% of the equipment you need to be successful in selling private RELPs.** The mind-set and skills of a RELP superstar are limitlessly transferable, not just among the different public RELP types, but across the whole spectrum of real estate investments and far beyond.

The only major factor you're missing is how to handle the prospect's CPA, which, as we suggested, is critical in private placements, but a non-issue in most public sales. To coin a phrase: We're coming to that.

PROSPECTING FOR THE SELECT SIXTY

First, let's talk about the psychology. A private RELP prospecting program *is different* from the one we suggested for your start-up efforts in public partnerships. There, we advocated picking a RELP that you loved and making the same number of presentations every day, starting in your "natural market" — your existing account book. The object of that exercise was to get you presenting RELPs in a systematic, non-anxiety-producing way.

Beyond that, we suggested restricting your "cold" prospecting to the pension market, where the tickets are big enough to warrant the effort. Prospecting "cold" in the pension market is also good practice for a private RELP sales campaign. You tend to be talking with the same kind of top-management and entrepreneurial types you'll encounter when showing private placements.

Most salespeople don't have enough private RELP prospects on the books to sustain any kind of real private RELP prospecting effort. Even accounts who are (or should be) private RELP prospects may be so important to you that you don't want to jeopardize the relationship by practicing something you don't really understand on them. So **you pretty much have to commit yourself to a "cold" prospecting effort.** That's daunting, sure, but the goal of this whole program is, after all, to change the character of your book.

Prospecting people you don't know with products you don't know well has to be the most anxiety-producing situation you can subject yourself to. You have to find an effective way to desensitize yourself to the anxiety, or you're going to fail to complete your prospecting program. How on earth do you do that? If you've been reading this book carefully, and really taking it to heart, you already know:

MAKE A NUMBERS GAME OUT OF IT.

You're going to establish a "baseline" prospecting program, in which you contact (in a very specific way which we'll describe in a minute) a set number of people every working day for a year.

It's important that you devote no more than an hour a day to this program and that you budget no additional business from it in your plans for the year. The object is to prevent the program from disturbing the conduct of your regular business — and to insure that all the revenue produced by the program will be completely incremental. It just won't work any other way. If you're going to look to the program for needed income, you put all the anxiety back into it.

For one hour, turn your mind off and do the program. You don't care about how many sales you make, or how much money you earn. **Just be concerned with completing your calls every day.** Make the calls, and the sales will take care of themselves.

In its purest form, this program calls for you to attempt to contact ten preselected people each working day. (If the secretary won't put you through, or the prospect hangs up on you, that still counts as one of your ten calls.) Remember that you want to **reward yourself for completing the behavior that leads to change** — you still get a sticker for your helmet.

If you work the program every day for a year, you'll try to contact about 2,200 people whom you will qualify harder than you've ever qualified anyone in your career. The prospect/contact ratio will be miniscule — if you end up with more than about sixty real prospects, it'll be a lot.

On the other hand, these "Select Sixty" prospects will be so well qualified that the conversion ratio of prospects to clients will be astronomical — something on the order of one in three, if not higher. So the "Select Sixty" prospects will yield twenty new clients. Over the course of a year, each one can give you one referral, who also makes an investment.

If forty people buy $50,000 in private placements (about 1/2 a unit, in most deals), you'll have $2,000,000 in sales in about a year and probably earn yourself an extra $75,000. But that's not the point.

The point is that if you can complete this prospecting program, you'll find yourself in the top 1% of all RELP salespeople in the United States. You will radically alter the character of your account book, and you'll be dealing with a class of accounts you may have thought you'd never crack.

You start by selecting at random, from at least a dozen different professional directories (so that you don't weaken later on thinking you've picked a "bad list"), about 3,000 names of people you can drive to see. Obviously, you only want lists with names *and* addresses *and* phone numbers. You're trying to accumulate, in descending order of desirability, business owners/entrepreneurs, top executives of small-to-mid-size companies and officers of larger companies. *No doctors.* This program is rigorous enough without subjecting yourself to that madness.

(What's that you say? You live all the way down in Brownsville, Texas, and the nearest library with extensive directories is at the SMU Business School in Dallas? Doesn't seem likely, but no matter. Saddle up and ride. We're giving you an absolutely foolproof way to move your whole career to a new level, and you're whining about a $100 plane ride? Knock it off.)

Four days before you start your one-year program, pick ten

names from as many lists, and write them a letter that sounds something like this:

Dear _____:

(Name of your firm) is active in the underwriting of private, tax-advantaged real estate investments. Here in the Brownsville office of (firm), I make a particular effort to specialize in this type of investment.

My experience is that we are successful in identifying each year between four and six genuinely superior trans-actions of this kind. When we do, I would like to bring them to your attention, if you feel this would be appro-priate for you.

I will call you very shortly to determine your interest in this investment area.

Sincerely,

(You'll want to clear the letter with your compliance peo-ple before you start sending it out. We must be mindful of the proprieties.)

Now, calendar those ten names for four business days from today. On the next day, send out ten more, and calendar those for a four-business-day lag. Same thing the third day.

On Day Four, in addition to sending out ten more letters, you call the first ten people. Invariably, you reach a secretary, who quite properly wants to know what the call is in refer-ence to. And that's when you say — *truthfully,* because this is why you sent the letter in the first place:

"We've had some correspondence about his income tax situation."

Yes, you're right: That's pretty strong. Maybe our children will live in a better world — a world where, when the salesperson is asked what it's in reference to, he can say, "I have wonderful things for Mr. Jones to invest in." And the secretary will say, "Oh, good!," and put you through. But not today. Today, this is what it will take to get you through. And will it ever. (Incidentally, if you don't get through, and the secretary will not suggest a better time for you to call, forget this prospect. But, the call counts toward your numerical prospecting objective.)

When the prospect comes on the line, you can say:

SUPERSTAR: *Good morning, Mr. Jones, this is Jim Superstar with Millbrook Securities. I wrote to you last week to introduce our services in the area of real estate investments. May I ask if you've invested in real estate private placements before?*

This question will draw responses which have two things in common:

(1) You'll hear the same "dirty dozen" answers over and over again.
(2) Without exception, the answers have nothing to do with reality; they are intended to get rid of you.

The idea now is for you to **say something, calmly and confidently, that stands some chance of shaking up the prospect's thinking . . . and then, go right back to your original question.**

Here are two examples:

PROSPECT: *I already have a broker.*

SUPERSTAR: *I was sure you would, Mr. Jones. Nearly all my clients have a good broker they rely on for traditional investments. I specialize in our real estate investments, and that's a full-time job. Have you ever invested in real estate private placements, Mr. Jones?*

Or

PROSPECT: *I'm not interested.*

SUPERSTAR: (With your biggest smile, which can be heard clearly) *Mr. Jones, my career involves finding people the right tax-advantaged investments . . . and I've never yet met anybody who wasn't interested in his after-tax investment results. Have you ever invested in real estate private placements, Mr. Jones?*

The prospect was not thinking about what he said. It was just "white noise," designed to get you off the phone. But the next thing he heard from you was an extremely poised, confident voice saying something quite intelligent . . . and asking the same question again. Once in a while he'll give you a real answer.

Here's another example of "white noise:"

PROSPECT: *No, no, tax shelters are finished. Congress put them out of business.*

SUPERSTAR: *That's why we only underwrite programs where the real estate economics are the main thing and the tax benefits just help out. Have you ever invested in real estate private placements, Mr. Jones?*

Do you see where we're going with this? Never mind what the other dirty dozen "white noise" objections are (they change with the seasons, anyway). When you start the prospecting program, just keep a notebook of each "white noise" objection you hear first on each call. Some of them will buffalo you at first, of course, but that's all right — the year is young.

The third time you hear any "white noise" objection, and you're not yet easily able to slide by it in the manner described above, stop. Call you internal wholesaler, or one from the private RELP. Tell him what you're doing, get a quick answer that's consistent with the style we're describing, and get back on the phone. It's only a game, after all.

All we're trying to do is answer the non-objection quietly and confidently, and reload the question, "Have you ever invested in real estate private placements, Mr. Jones?" And the idea is to just keep doing that until the prospect

(1) hangs up,
(2) says "No," or
(3) says "Yes."

Of those three outcomes, we'd prefer that he didn't hang up. But "No" and "Yes" are equally acceptable. Here's how.

PROSPECT: *No.*

SUPERSTAR: *Have you not invested in real estate private placements because you've never seriously looked at them? Or because you feel your financial situation isn't strong enough?*

Why those two choices? No particular reason. (Oh, perhaps the second choice is there to tell you if you've picked a wrong prospect. But you'll still need to probe to see if he's really disqualified.) What you really hope will happen is that he'll blurt out a third reason — one all his own:

PROSPECT: (With rage) *I lost $50,000 in an oil deal in 1981!*

Now we're getting somewhere. If the prospect rejects your two choices and sticks in one of his own, it's probably a pretty real objection, and now you can start communicating.

SUPERSTAR: *Well, oil and gas has always been a cyclical commodity, and 1981 was really the top of the cycle. Real estate, on the other hand, can be an investment for all seasons. Would you like to look at a sensible real estate investment, Mr. Jones?*

Remember, nobody's really mad at real estate. So if a prospect is really griped about something, it isn't real estate . . . and it isn't you. Let him *ventilate*, then *validate* his feelings, and steer him back in the right direction. Now, if he still says "No," meaning that he won't look at a sensible real estate investment, ask him "Why?" Listen very carefully to the answer.

(Remember, the object of this inquiry is not to keep him on the phone. It's to find out whether he will be one of the fortunate few — the one or two people a week — who make it into your "Select Sixty" prospects this year.)

PROSPECT: *I just told you. I had a terrible experience in tax shelters.*

SUPERSTAR: (Very gently) *Mr. Jones, have you noticed that, even though you had that bad experience in tax shelters, the government hasn't stopped taxing you?*

(Alternative 1)

PROSPECT: (Sheepishly) *All right. I see what you mean. What have you got?*

(The technical answer to the question is: You've got a "suspect" on the phone. He isn't qualified to be one of your "Select Sixty" prospects yet, but he is starting to make noises which give one cause to hope. You'll learn what you say to "What have you got?" in just a minute.)

(Alternative 2)

PROSPECT: (Not at all sheepishly) *I don't know what you're talking about. Leave me alone.*

SUPERSTAR: *Goodbye, Mr. Jones.*

The purpose of keeping your "white noise" notebook is so you start to develop easy, practiced answers to repetitive zingers. You can do that if you're just playing out a numbers game. But if your ego is even the least bit invested in these calls, you're a gone goose.

YOU'RE THE DIRECTOR: THE PROSPECTS ARE THE DANCERS

Are you starting to see why this process is called "Disqualifying The Prospect?" **The whole key to making the method work is to feel in control of the situation, and simply not to care.** Nobody can do that for more than an hour a day; most people can't even do it for that long. The salesperson who wins at this game is the one who is in possession of the cold reality that somewhere between 48 and 49 of the 50 people he calls every week are going to fail to make the cut, because of some sad, misguided, uncontrollable impulse of theirs that the salesperson can't change.

Have you ever seen the show or the movie *A Chorus Line?* It's about a large number of hopeful dancers who are trying out for a very small number of spots in a new show. The key character is the director, sitting down in the audience behind the footlights, auditioning this legion of performers. Their fate is in his hands; he absolutely controls their destinies. *A Chorus Line* is the perfect metaphor for "Disqualifying The Prospect," in exactly this way:

THE RELP SUPERSTAR BELIEVES
THAT HE IS THE DIRECTOR, AND THAT
HIS FIFTY CALLS A WEEK ARE THE DANCERS.
THE RELP WASHOUT, TRY AS HE MAY,
THINKS THE OTHER WAY AROUND.

See it that way, and you're virtually guaranteed to be able to complete this program. Fail to see it, and, no matter what other noble disciplines you have, "Disqualifying The Prospect" will bury you.

You just keep gently brushing aside each objection the prospect has, and you go on asking, "Do you invest in real estate private placements?" or "Would you like to look at a sensible real estate investment?" This process moves the prospect slowly toward the point where he either hangs up on you or says "Yes." Once or twice a week, it will be the latter.

And then you can say:

SUPERSTAR: *That's great, Mr. Jones. I'd really like to introduce you to my firm's real estate investments.*
    I find that we're able to generate four to six clearly superior transactions each year, and, when I find my next one, I'd be pleased to show it to you.

That's an extremely difficult thing for a *prospect* to say no to. If he does, disqualify him.

You see, the intelligent prospect will have recognized that you're only talking about four to six opportunities a year. You've said, in effect: "I sit here all year long, looking at everything the firm is doing. Once every couple or three months, I spot something I have absolute confidence in. On those very rare occasions, I'd like to call you and tell you about it."

It's virtually impossible for a sensible prospect to say no to this. A reasonable man has got to realize, at this point, that he's talking to a quiet, confident professional. He may even feel a flicker of the realization that **you're qualifying him,** not the other way around. At any rate, he surely sees that you've said you'll call him as few as four and as many as six times in a whole year — and only when you have an absolutely first-rate story to tell. The person who accepts this, and who agrees to listen, is skating perilously close to becoming a real prospect.

When a prospect says "Yes," that he'll listen for a while to the few stories you'll want to tell him, you're almost finished. Here's your sign-off:

SUPERSTAR: *Thanks, Mr. Jones. I've taken up quite enough of your time, and I appreciate your speaking with me.*

      Incidentally, since I usually work on private real estate offerings, they generally involve a commitment of $50,000 or more.

      You pay that in over four or five years, of course, you'll be getting a growing stream of tax-sheltered income and, hopefully, a property that is appreciating.

      But I guess what I want to ask you is: Is that kind of commitment, in and of itself, too big a bite?

When someone says flatly "that's too much money," under any circumstances, you can do one of three things:

(1) chuck the lead;

(2) explain that, once in a while, there's a high-quality offering that doesn't require such a heavy outlay of capital, and then go back to him at some point with a leveraged public deal; or

(3) put the prospect card away, and try him again in a couple of months on municipal bonds, or annuities, or something else.

But if the prospect says $50,000 isn't too much for the right deal — and people who feel that way are very proud to tell you so — you have yourself one terrific prospect, one of your "Select Sixty."

Do not ask him a whole laundry list of financial planning-type questions, and *do not* ask him what kind of deal he wants to buy (you're making the deal selections, remember?).

Just say:

SUPERSTAR: *Thanks again, Mr. Jones. Whenever I call back it will just be to ask for four minutes of your time to run by you the bare bones of an investment idea.*

                I'll confirm that in a letter to you. Thanks again for your time.

Do not try to present an investment on this call. If he asks, "What have you got?" say that you've nothing in particular at the moment, which is why you have time to make introductory calls like this. When you do have an interesting idea, you'll be sure to let him know. Then get off the phone. He was only testing you, anyway, to see whether, with a little encouragement, you'd turn into just another peddler. Besides, you know something he doesn't know:

YOU'LL HAVE YOUR NEXT GREAT IDEA
TEN DAYS LATER.

That's about as much time as you want to let go by. Meantime, you'll have written him a confirming letter reiterating your four-to-six transactions a year scenario. Restate that you'll only ask to speak to him for four minutes next time you call, and thank him again for his time.

THE FOUR-MINUTE FOLLOW-UP

Ten days later, you'll call him, and get the secretary again. You can truthfully tell her that (a) her boss is expecting your call, and (b) that he knows you only need four minutes of his time.

If she says he's in conference, or away from the office, you have an opportunity to ask her to help you pick the most likely spot in his calendar when he might have four minutes to spare. You are speaking to her expertise and her competence in maintaining control of his schedule. Instead of butting heads with her and creating an adversary relationship, you appeal to her sense of what she does best. That's pretty hard to resist.

When you talk to your prospect, remind him that you're just going to need four minutes, and ask him if he can grab a pencil and jot down some figures. That's a really effective way of requalifying the prospect and of getting him working with you.

For the first two minutes, in maybe five to seven sentences, you'll tell your prospect about the real estate, the general partner, the strategy and perhaps one or two outstanding deal points. Work this presentation out carefully and time it before you use it.

Then, you'll ask him to take the pencil and make four-column headings: "year," "capital contributions," "taxable income (or loss)" and, "cash flow." Just run through the years of the pay-in period. Sum the numbers for him in each column.

Now all you have to do is ask him, "Without knowing any of the other details, does the outline of the transaction sound reasonable to you, or does it miss what you're looking for in some way?" That's a very carefully phrased question. If he says anything like, "Well, it's not enough information . . . I need to know more . . . it could be appropriate . . . ," or any answer that isn't actively hostile, **the prospect is already about one-third closed.** (On the other hand, if he says he was looking for something more along the lines of a one-time, nine-to-one write-off, you can tear up the card.)

Now you're at the most critical juncture of this call, where the great majority of would-be RELP superstars go wrong. If the prospect doesn't immediately take violent exception to the transaction, most salespeople ask if they can come out and see him and tell him the story. Asking for the interview now is *absolutely* the wrong thing to do.

The reason is that you're letting your enthusiasm sweep you forward into a position that causes more heartbreak and discouragement to the private placement salesperson than all other sources combined. You're setting yourself up to go out there and tell your story with honesty, warmth and conviction. Then, you'll listen in horror as the client sits back and says, "Well, it sounds all right, I guess, but I have to have my CPA review it." And, of course, the sale disappears without a trace.

Instead, here's an absolutely foolproof *superqualifier* to use at the end of the second call, after your prospect has heard the outline, jotted down the numbers, and indicated that, so far, it sounds like it might make sense:

SUPERSTAR: *Mr. Jones, looking at what you've written down . . . looking at the size of the commitment, and at the economic benefits . . . let me ask you one more question.*

                Is this the kind of investment decision you're going to make on your own, or will you normally rely on the advice of an accountant or an attorney?

The single most common mistake would-be private placement salespeople make is attempting an end-around on the CPA. That's probably because they're pretty sure that they can successfully present a transaction to an investor, but fear that a CPA is going to do them in with a lot of technical questions.

But since you're never going to go out on a private placement sales call without a backup person, you never have to worry about that. Now you can focus correctly on what you know is the right thing to do: Bring the accountant into the play on *your* terms and *your* timing, if he's going to come into the play at all. He often is, so this is the ideal way to handle him.

On seven or eight out of ten occasions the conversation will go like this:

PROSPECT: *No way I buy anything that big or that complex without my CPA.*

SUPERSTAR: *That's great, Mr. Jones. I'm glad you have a good accountant you can rely on. I'm going to order out an offering memorandum for you, and one for him. And what I'd like us to do now is to start working on a mutually convenient time for the three of us to get together.*

This is the ultimate test of the prospect's seriousness, as of the end of the second call. (The ultimate test at the end of the first call was the question about whether $50,000 is too big a bite.)

You *can* allow the prospect to say, "Well, let's wait until we've reviewed the book first, to see if the meeting is necessary." That's not an unreasonable position for him to take. But then, don't go see him until you know you're going to meet with him *and* the CPA, or until the CPA has signed off on the deal. **Once you know the CPA's blessing is critical to the prospect's decision, never present yourself, in a selling**

mode, to the prospect alone. If you do so, by definition, you are in a sales interview in which you can't close. There's no valid reason to do that to yourself, ever.

If the prospect says anything that sounds like, "No, I don't want to meet with you and him," or, "You needn't send the CPA the book," or anything similar, disqualify him. He's told you that he's not going to do business with you. In the space of a couple of minutes, he told you he'd need his CPA's guidance. But then he didn't want you to meet the CPA, or didn't want him to see the book on your deal. Pass. You're the director. Dismiss the dancer.

You may never find out why he wouldn't play straight with you, so don't be concerned. Just take comfort from the fact that you didn't go charging out to see him and waste your time telling him a story he was never going to buy. Go on with the prospecting process, because the success of the process is inevitable.

CLEARING THE CPA HURDLE

Now, suppose your prospect says, "Yes." What if he accepts your suggestion that he and his CPA read the book and that the three of you get together? Well, now you have got one of your "Select Sixty," one terrifically well-qualified prospect. To start with, he has $200 invested in finding out more about your transaction, because that's about the accountant's charge to read the book and come to the meeting. If your prospect wants to pay that, he's a great prospect! And, at this point, he's about 50% closed.

You order out the memoranda, and, after a couple of phone calls back and forth, you set up a meeting for three o'clock, a week away. (Where the prospect makes an honest effort on this, but conflicting schedules prevent it, go for a four-way conference call with you, the prospect, the CPA and your backup person. This tactic may also work where they don't want to decide on whether to have a meeting until after they read the book.) Immediately send off confirming notes to both parties, indicating that the book is coming under separate cover.

Two days before the actual meeting is to take place, you'll call the prospect to reconfirm. Never fail to do this. It will give the prospect a chance to say one of two things. The first thing he may say is any variation of "Well, I'm glad you called. I'd actually meant to call you, because it won't be necessary to have the meeting. My CPA read the book, and he's advised me not to buy it." Your line is:

SUPERSTAR: *Did he think it wasn't right for you, or did he think there was something fundamentally wrong with the transaction?*

What you're solving for here is the "smoking gun" issue. Remember our fundamental rule that anyone can tell you why your RELP isn't right *for him,* but nobody can tell you that your RELP is objectively, fatally flawed.

Your instinctive reaction of asking a very pointed question in a totally unflustered way also has, in and of itself, a fairly telling psychological effect on the prospect. He expected you to whine, moan, argue and generally try to draw him into further conversation about a subject to which he's already closed his mind. But you didn't.

Generally, the prospect won't have a particularly crisp answer to your question; the accountant said ix-nay, and that was good enough for him. So he mumbles something vague which usually centers on some perceived flaw in the deal. (On those rare occasions when his answer is a statement of why it isn't right for him, remember that he has told you what he *will* buy.) That's when you say:

SUPERSTAR: *Mr. Jones, I honestly believe he's misunderstood that aspect of the transaction. May I have your permission to call him in order to straighten this out?*

Of course, if the prospect says "No" to this eminently reasonable request, he's totally disqualified himself. Quite clearly, he's told you he isn't going to do business with you, and he's probably never going to tell you why. "C'est la guerre," thinks the superstar, chalking up another hashmark on his inexorable road to success.

Far more often, in the great tradition of "Let's you and him fight," the prospect will say, "Sure . . . go ahead and call him if you like." He'll do this for the same reason J.P. Morgan told Andrew Carnegie he'd have gladly paid another $100 million to buy U.S. Steel: "If only to be rid of you." And that's fine.

Because now you can call the accountant, in an attitude of total bewilderment, and say:

SUPERSTAR: *I talked to our mutual client, Mr. Jones, about a transaction I recommended called Brixnstix Apartments. He mentioned that you had recommended against it, apparently on the grounds that . . .*

   (Fill in your own garbled version of the prospect's garbled objection).

   Was that an accurate statement of your concern?

   (Be sure to use the word "client," even though it's only prospectively correct. And, stress the word "apparently" very hard, in a general tone of disbelief.)

The CPA can only respond in one of two ways. He can blow a lot of fast-talking smoke at you. The signal is they don't want to do business with you, and the prospect is letting the CPA be the bad guy. You'll be able to tell just by listening to the pace and tone of how he speaks: curt, abrupt, and dismissive. (As always, the words don't matter.)

Or he'll actually say, "No, that's not quite right. I specifically object to . . . ," and he'll then voice a genuine criticism of the deal. Never mind what it is. *Do not try to respond to it.* Just say:

SUPERSTAR: *Mr. CPA, I don't feel able to respond to that as rigorously as you'd want. You and Mr. Jones have obviously invested a fair amount of time researching this RELP. Will you invest another minute and a half so that I can patch us through to my real estate department in* (headquarters city)? *I'd like them to respond to you directly.*

If he says "No," he's disqualified himself and his client. If he says "Yes," he's still alive. You'll want to patch him right through to your backup person, who will powder his objection. (If you don't know physically how to do this on your phone, stop reading immediately and learn how.) When the CPA acknowledges that the backup person's answer solves his problem, immediately ask if you can reschedule the three-way meeting with him, the client and you.

Often, he'll say, "No, it's not necessary." You've removed his objection, so he no longer opposes the investment. Ask if he wants you to tell the client, or if he'll do it. Usually he'll say that the client wants to hear it from him. Say "Thanks," and ask him when you can call the client to make an appointment to complete the paperwork. This move puts the pressure on the CPA to call the client relatively quickly.

Throughout this process, you have never moved from your desk and never failed to have the maximum potential control over events. You did not spend a lot of travel time, frustration and agony getting battered from pillar to post by this prospect and his CPA. You have to save your strength for positive sales situations.

Let's go back to reconfirming the appointment. The only other possible outcome (beside the CPA turning the deal down) is relatively positive:

PROSPECT: *Well, we've looked at the book. We have a lot of serious reservations. The section on risks and conflicts of interest is awfully scary. These fees are really something. But we're prepared to have the meeting. Come ahead.*

How can you not love this guy? He's told you that he and the CPA have all kinds of hang-ups about your RELP, but *they want to see you anyway.* What, therefore, is he really saying?

> *"I want to be convinced.*
> *I want to believe."*

Wonderful. This sale is 80% closed, and you have never moved from your desk, never gotten your hopes up, and not taken more than a couple of minutes away from the conduct of your regular business.

Then, on the day of the appointment, you can finally take the time to see this prospect, because you've qualified the daylights out of him. You've smoked out his accountant. They both read the offering memorandum, and both of them want to talk to you. Only when you've accomplished all this can you really feel you have a genuinely qualified private placement prospect.

What do you do in the next thirty seconds after the prospect confirms the meeting? Right. Call for a backup person. Make sure you have the third-party expert waiting to field the inevitable question you can't answer at the day and time of your appointment.

THE MEET AND THE CLOSE

What you do at the meeting is pretty much up to you. As a suggestion, simply ask them if they want to go right to Q&A, or if they'll give you three or four minutes to review the essence of the deal. If they elect the latter, go over the three to five key points you've previously discussed, stressing the aspects of the transaction which you feel are unique, or which make this RELP, *in your view,* particularly appropriate for the prospect's situation, as you understand it. Be very conscious of the issue of tone, and try to feel for the emotional tenor of the meeting.

Be sure to work into your presentation the fact that this investment is one of your four to six "hits of the year." This phraseology has the subtle effect of enhancing the importance of the deal and your importance as a salesperson.

Then you arrive at Q&A. Again, you'll gradually know more and more of the answers as you work your way up the learning curve. But never mind that. The critical moment comes when they raise an issue, and you say, "I don't know." Go to your backup person. When your expert has answered the question satisfactorily, you can do your famous routine, "Now, before we let Mr. Backup off the phone, are there any other questions or problems . . . ?" (See Chapter 14.)

This technique works even better in private placements than in public RELPs, largely because private transactions usually have a much shorter time fuse until the offering is closed. You have a real need to accelerate the decision, making the "now or never" approach more appropriate and, therefore, more acceptable. Then, if necessary, isolate the blocking objection, and the sale is closed.

The approach to private placement sales outlined in this chapter is totally consistent with the general theory that runs through this whole book. You stress a prospecting procedure, in the belief that product knowledge will come in time.

Prospecting wealthy people with large-ticket, complex products is anxiety-producing enough. Don't complicate the process by grinding up your time and energy on people who haven't gone through a lot to get to meet you and the RELP you love. In other words, don't raise the chances that you'll fail to complete a prospecting program. Allow prospects to disqualify themselves. Concentrate on developing a very small number of qualified prospects. Remember: They're the dancers; you're the director.

STARTING THE REFERRAL MACHINE

Let's spend a little time on referrals. RELPs in general, and private placements in particular, are phenomenally conducive to producing referrals. In private placements, you have different opportunities to ask for a referral. The first can be the point when the prospect is filling out the closing documents. Here's a script you can play around with and adapt to your own personal style:

> *"I know I've said to you several times that I can only find a small handful of transactions of this calibre each year. It takes virtually a full-time effort to identify them and to bring them quickly to my clients' attention when they occur.*
>
> *So the good news, I think, is that my clients get a lot of screening work done for them, and end up seeing only the best transactions available.*
>
> *The bad news, at least for me, is that I have virtually no time to work on finding new clients. So I rely on my existing clients to help me reach new people.*
>
> *Can either of you (client or his CPA) think of someone for whom this transaction would be particularly appropriate?"*

This approach is a very disarming and perfectly consistent with everything you've said about yourself and the way you conduct your business. You catch both the client and the CPA together, at the moment when their shared enthusiasm for the transaction is at its zenith: just when they've bought it.

The second opportunity you have to ask for a referral is the next time one of your "hit" RELPs shows up. You have the chance to call the CPA *directly* and go through your speech that the new RELP is one of your four-to-six. Ask if he'd like to suggest others among his clientele who might be interested. He'll ask to see the memorandum first. Of course, that is your signal to set up a subsequent meeting, being sure a backup person will be able to assist you.

Prospecting CPAs directly is hard work as a cold approach. But, once a CPA has participated in a favorable decision to invest with you, he should be considered just as much a part of your clientele as your actual investor. See that he receives copies of all correspondence. Call him to report favorable developments, and work to keep the lines of communication open. You'll be amply rewarded.

SUMMARY

- **Sooner or later, every RELP superstar wants to try his hand at private placements.**

- **The income of a financial communicator/salesperson is an absolute function of the incomes of his clients.**

- **Private RELPs are the most efficient discipline you can bring to your prospecting efforts to keep you focused on the kinds of prospects who will have the greatest impact on your career.**

- **Private RELPs, far from being complex, are focused and specific. Still,**

- **You'll always be asked a question you can't answer. So, never work without a backup person.**

- **If you've accepted the attitudes and techniques in this book, you have 90% of the equipment you need to be successful in selling private RELPs.**

- Private RELPs are big enough tickets to warrant cold prospecting. Write to ten people a day, and follow up by phone. If you can't sustain ten, work down to a sustainable, "baseline" number.

- Work through a prospect's "white noise" objections until he either hangs up or agrees to talk to you for four minutes next time you call.

- Qualify specifically, using $50,000 as an average investment.

- On your second call, ask a prospect to write the numbers down. Then ask if the CPA will be involved, and only see them together.

- Reconfirm the appointment. Be prepared to call the CPA to work through an objection. Use your backup person.

- At the meeting, ask for permission to reiterate the reasons behind your personal enthusiasm for the RELP. Then wait for the question you can't answer, go to the backup person, and close.

- Ask for referrals twice: once at the initial closing, and again from the CPAs when your next "hit" RELP comes out.